The Tomb of the Artisan God

A Univocal Book

Drew Burk, Consulting Editor

Univocal Publishing was founded by Jason Wagner and Drew Burk as an independent publishing house specializing in artisanal editions and translations of texts spanning the areas of cultural theory, media archeology, continental philosophy, aesthetics, anthropology, and more. In May 2017, Univocal ceased operations as an independent publishing house and became a series with its publishing partner the University of Minnesota Press.

Univocal authors include:

Miguel Abensour
Judith Balso
Jean Baudrillard
Philippe Beck
Simon Critchley
Fernand Deligny
Jacques Derrida
Vinciane Despret
Georges Didi-Huberman
Jean Epstein
Vilém Flusser
Barbara Glowczewski
Évelyne Grossman
Félix Guattari
David Lapoujade
François Laruelle

David Link
Sylvère Lotringer
Michael Marder
Serge Margel
Quentin Meillassoux
Friedrich Nietzsche
Peter Pál Pelbart
Jacques Rancière
Lionel Ruffel
Michel Serres
Gilbert Simondon
Étienne Souriau
Isabelle Stengers
Eugene Thacker
Siegfried Zielinski

The Tomb of the Artisan God

On Plato's *Timaeus*

SERGE MARGEL
Translated by Philippe Lynes

A Univocal Book

University of Minnesota Press
Minneapolis
London

Cet ouvrage a bénéficié du soutien des Programmes d'aide à la publication de l'Institut français. This book received a publication grant from the Institut Français.

Originally published in French as *Le tombeau du dieu artisan,* copyright 1995 by Les Éditions de Minuit

Published by the University of Minnesota Press
111 Third Avenue South, Suite 290
Minneapolis, MN 55401-2520
http://www.upress.umn.edu

Printed in the United States of America on acid-free paper

The University of Minnesota is an equal-opportunity educator and employer.

24   23   22   21   20   19   9   8   7   6   5   4   3   2   1

Library of Congress Cataloging-in-Publication Data
Names: Margel, Serge, author.
Title: The tomb of the artisan god : on Plato's Timaeus / Serge Margel ; translated by Philippe Lynes.
Other titles: Tombeau du dieu artisan. English
Description: Minneapolis : University of Minnesota Press, 2019. | Series: A Univocal book | Includes bibliographical references.
Identifiers: LCCN 2018024551 (print) | ISBN 978-1-5179-0642-9 (pb)
Subjects: LCSH: Plato. Timaeus. | Cosmology, Ancient.
Classification: LCC B387 .M3713 2019 (print) | DDC 113—dc23
LC record available at https://lccn.loc.gov/2018024551

For my mother

Let me give one example of the many from which I could choose. Suppose that I am watching the break of day. I predict that the sun is about to rise. What I see is present, but what I foretell is future. I do not mean that the sun is future, for it already exists, but that its rise is future, because it has not yet happened. But I could not foretell the sunrise unless I had a picture of it in my mind, just as I have at this moment while I am speaking of it. Yet the dawn, which I see in the sky, is not the sunrise, although it precedes it; nor is the picture which I have in my mind the sunrise. But both the dawn and my mental picture are seen in the present, and it is from them that I am able to predict the sunrise, which is future. The future, then, is not yet; it is not at all; and if it is not at all, it cannot possibly be seen. But it can be foretold from things which are present, because they exist now and can therefore be seen.

In what way, then, do you, Ruler of all that you have created, reveal the future to the souls of men? You have revealed it to your prophets. But how do you reveal the future to us when, for us, the future does not exist? Is it that you only reveal present signs of things that are to come? For it is utterly impossible that things which do not exist should be revealed. The means by which you do this is far beyond our understanding. I have not the strength to comprehend this mystery, and by my own power I never shall. But in your strength I shall understand it, when you grant me the grace to see, sweet Light of the eyes of my soul.

—*Saint Augustine*, Confessions *XI, 18–19*

Contents

Publisher's Note

The original French publication of this text was preceded by a long foreword written by Jacques Derrida, now translated and published in English as *Advances* (University of Minnesota Press, 2017).

Preface to the English Edition

Plato's *Timaeus* is a great metaphysical text on time and eternity, being and nothingness, the finite and the infinite, but it is also a moral text, thematizing the relations between the soul and the body. In *The Tomb of the Artisan God*, I attempted to articulate these two great philosophical registers, metaphysics and morals, departing from a hypothesis concerning the demiurge's body, its anthropomorphic attributes, its productive capacities and regulatory functions in the order of the world. The demiurge's body is no mere cosmological metaphor for the living body; it is also the site of its destruction, dissolution, and disappearance. The demiurge's body is torn between the paradigm of the ideas and the horizon of a finitude, by which the world he created or assembled is ceaselessly threatened with an imminent death.

All the problems taken on in this text, which was my first published book, more than twenty years ago, have never ceased to concern me, returning to haunt me like so many questions that still structure and orient my work, research and teaching. The metaphysical question of time has remained my principal question, which I have since expanded and developed through other philosophers, from Augustine to Husserl. Being and time, space and time, memory and time, eternity and time, the end of time— all these notions developed in the *Timaeus* became for me nomadic concepts that spanned the history of philosophy. The other great question bears upon the ontological status of the body, the body of the demiurge, the body of the gods, the body of the world, but also what the first Christians will call the body of flesh, a living body that survives in perpetually experiencing the trial of its own death. Plato opens up a field of study: the relations and distinctions between the soul and the body. The body is separate from the soul but at the same time suffers the affectations of the body; it directs the body all the while being submitted to its constraints. What is a body? This is the *Timaeus*'s question, which Plato dramatizes by attributing a body to the demiurge, whose ontological status will become increasingly decisive in the history of philosophy, particularly in Christianity and its dogma of incarnation.

The *Timaeus* is a great metaphysical text, and one that has long rivaled the *Parmenides* for first place in Platonic schools. It is a metaphysical text, but it is also a fiction, a tale or fable. Metaphysics and morals weave together metaphysics and fiction in this text. In other words, the *Timaeus*'s metaphysics is not thinkable without the invention of a "likely tale" that comes from afar, outside Greece, and is told, transmitted, and written. Metaphysics is not a fiction, but there can be no metaphysics without fiction, or without the fictional space of a discourse that ideally reconstructs an origin of the world, time, the soul, and the body. It is not the question of the literary that is posed here, but rather of writing. Metaphysical discourse must also be thought of as a text, which is written. It must not only be commented upon—and the *Timaeus* will have been one of the most commented-upon texts in philosophy—but also followed through and reinvented in its writing. Fiction, the tale, likeliness represent so many metaphysical fates of an ideal order of the world, condemned to the imminence of its disappearance or threatened with self-destruction. The history of metaphysics is shot through with this tension between writing and ideality, of which the *Timaeus* sets the scene through the paradoxical notion of the demiurge's body.

These reflections on the body, the body of the gods, and the demiurgic body were for me the first opening toward the question of the religious. The body as the site of the inscription of a tale, such as we find it in early Christianity, has developed throughout history: body of flesh, witnessing body, body of avowal, suffering body, with its instrumental functions and powers, but also a body subject to different secretions (tears, blood, pus), which represent so many traces of this paradoxical site—opened up and thematized by the *Timaeus*—between the transcendence of the ideas and the immanence of a writing. From the theomorphism of the human body to the anthropomorphism of the divine body, the *Timaeus* in my eyes remains the insurmountable horizon of any metaphysical thought of the body, of the relations and distinctions between the soul and the body. How do matters stand with Christianity, and Judeo-Christianity, on the horizon of a commentary on the *Timaeus*? How do matters stand with the other monotheistic religions, so-called religions of the book, before a reading of the *Timaeus*? Could Christianity have been invented, instituted—could it have survived without a certain understanding of the *Timaeus* and the inoperative body of the demiurge? This question remains open, subject to the rigorous study of texts, dogmas, and practices. It should be posed as such, all the while being articulated upon the great controversies of the Platonic and Neoplatonic commentators on the status of the *Timaeus* with respect to the *Parmenides*. We should once again, with respect to Christianity, bring face-to-face these two great texts of philosophy and thereby rethink the history of Western metaphysics, from Plotinus to Avicenna, Averroes, and Maimonides, from Saint Augustine to Saint Thomas Aquinas.

2017

Introduction

We no longer count the interpretations of the *Timaeus*. From Aristotle to Philo, Plotinus to Proclus, to Leibniz and Schelling, from last century's philologists to the latest scholarly translations, commentaries—line by line, passage by passage—are perpetually and regularly renewed.[1] And yet, everything seems to remain untouched in Plato's text, as if nothing had yet been said. One could then perhaps hope to take up the text anew and start all over. But this naive idea is far from our intention. Rather, we would prefer to tease out an aporia from this ampleness of interpretation, to describe a paradox in all the inexhaustible force of its formation, displacements, and inevitable attempts at its resolution. It will be a matter, in a single interpretive move, both of following the text to the letter, following as one tracks wild game, and inflicting a

---

1. We have used the following editions, translations, and commentaries: R. D. Archer-Hind, *The* Timaeus *of Plato, with Introduction and Notes* (London: Macmillan, 1888); A. E. Taylor, *A Commentary on Plato's* Timaeus (Oxford: Clarendon Press, 1928); Francis M. Cornford, *Plato's Cosmology: The* Timaeus *of Plato Translated with a Running Commentary* (London: Hackett, 1937); Plato, *Timée-Critias*, ed. Albert Rivaud (Paris: Les Belles Lettres, 1925); Plato, *Timée*, translation and notes by J. Moreau in *Œuvres complètes de Platon* (Paris: Pleiade, 1942); Luc Brisson, *Le même et l'autre dans la structure ontologique du* Timée *de Platon: Un commentaire systématique du "Timée" de Platon* (Paris: Klincksieck, 1974), and, by the same author, Plato, *Timée-Critias*, ed. and trans. Luc Brisson (Paris: Flammarion, 1999).

[TN: all English translations of the *Timaeus*, except where noted otherwise, will be drawn from Plato, *Timaeus*, trans. Donald J. Zeyl, in Plato, *Complete*

1

certain violence upon it, working the text to such an extent that it brings itself to its limit and remains at its state of aporia. We will thus attempt to problematize the paradoxical figures of the demiurge. While these figures are numerous, each is articulated around the same axis, that of his divine authority, productive force, and mimetic power. The text of the *Timaeus* would constitute the description and demonstration of this authority just as much as the account of its gradual destitution, up to the most radical limit of inoperativity. Plato's demiurge is an artisan god, an exemplary maker, a laborer, builder of an edifying work. But he is also an inoperative god, a powerless and dying god. We will make of the demiurge a hindered god, always on the verge of no longer being *capable* of representing the world he produces in the ideal image of the immortal gods. The demiurge will of course produce this world, from the dynamic assemblage of elementary corpuscles (earth, water, air and fire) to the regular revolutions of the planets, but the rational order of the world will nonetheless constitute an order *represented* by the demiurge, an order structurally dependent upon his own will.

The demiurge would not have created the primary elements he takes hold of to build the world through and through. Moreover,

---

Works, ed. John M. Cooper (Indianapolis: Hackett, 1997), 1224–91. Furthermore, all other translations of Plato will be drawn from this volume, henceforth abbreviated PCW. At the request of the author, certain English translations of Plato have been slightly modified (e.g., "elements" for "kinds," "omnitemporal" for "eternal"). All English translations of Aristotle will be drawn from *The Complete Works of Aristotle: The Revised Oxford Translation,* ed. Jonathan Barnes, 2 vols. (Princeton: Princeton University Press, 1984), henceforth abbreviated ACW. All English translations of the Presocratics will be drawn from *The Texts of Early Greek Philosophy: The Complete Fragments and Selected Testimonies of the Major Presocratics,* ed. and trans. Daniel W. Graham (Cambridge: Cambridge University Press, 2010), henceforth abbreviated TEGP. References will also be provided, following Margel's original text, to Hermann Diels's authoritative but now somewhat outdated anthology, *Die Fragmente der Vorsokratiker: Griechisch und Deutsch,* ed. Walther Kranz, 3 vols., 9th ed. (Berlin: Weidmannsche Verlagsbuchhandlung, 1960), henceforth abbreviated DK. All Presocratic fragments and testimonials will thus be referenced as Author (DK, *text number*; TEGP, *text number,* page number). Heraclitus's famed αἰών παῖς ἐστι παίζων πεσσεύων᾽ παιδὸς ἡ βασιληίη, for example, would be referenced Heraclitus (DK, *B 52*; TEGP, *154,* 178–79).]

2

as perfect as the world may be, and as pure as its order and harmony may be, the world in its elementary genesis will rest upon a *force of consummation* that devours it from within and spontaneously leads it toward a slow but certain death. The demiurge's cosmic representation (μίμησις) would consist in *idealizing* this gradual movement of consummation—not to definitively reduce this internal death principle, but to maintain this movement for a still indefinite but nonetheless already limited time, in an actual state of equilibrium and conservation. Thus, the figure of the demiurge is inscribed in a "likely account" (εἰκὼς λόγος) or in a "likely tale" or "likely story" (εἰκὼς μῦθος).[2] Timaeus's tale that Plato speaks of must be understood as a myth, fable, falsehood (ψεῦδος), but a noble (γενναῖος) falsehood, as the *Republic* will put it (III, 414a-c).[3] This fabulous tale will constitute the narration of a genesis. It will recount, recite, and describe how the demiurge begat the world. This fable will thus contain the *genesis of the demiurgic representation of the world*. However, if the narration of this fable can be deemed dishonest, it is not because its account is misleading, which would come down to making the demiurge a fundamentally perverse and willfully destructive god. Quite the contrary, this narrative falsehood issues from a structural fact. For, as we will see, the limits of this tale's likelihood will be determined

---

2. On the εἰκὼς λόγος, see 29c, 30b, 40e, 48d, 53d, 56a, 57d, 59d, 68b, 90e, and on the εἰκὼς μῦθος, see 29d, 59c, 68d. Cf. Bernd Witte, "Der EIKOS LOGOS in Platos Timaios: Beitrag zur Wissenschaftsmethode und Erkenntnistheorie des Späten Plato," *Archiv für Geschichte der Philosophie* 46 (1964): 1–16; E. Howald, "Εἰκὼς λόγος," *Hermes* 57 (1922): 63–79; and Pierre Hadot, "Physique et poésie dans le *Timée* de Platon," *Revue de Théologie et de Philosophie* 115 (1983): 118–23. As Cornford notes (*Plato's Cosmology*, 30), when Plato uses the expression εἰκὼς λόγος, he is thinking of the text of the *Timaeus* in the tradition of the great theogonic and cosmological poems. This is indeed how Hesiod (*Theogony*, line 27), Xenophanes (DK, B35; TEGP, 75, 126–27), and Parmenides (DK, B8; TEGP, 17, 218–19) designated their own philosophical poetry.

3. Let us specify that Plato will distinguish two levels of the lie: the real, authentic lie (τὸ . . . τῷ ὄντι ψεῦδος), the one committed in ignorance, and the purely verbal lie (τὸ ἐν τοῖς λόγοις), the latter definable as a good when produced for a good cause (*Republic*, II, 382b) (cf. J. Souihlé, "Notes sur le problème moral du mensonge et la pensée grecque," *Archives de Philosophies* 2, no. 3 [1924]: 64–65). It is thus this purely verbal lie that will constitute the noble lie of the *Timaeus*.

by the productive limits of the demiurge's representation.[4] The demiurge's mimetic powerlessness would forever risk reducing the rational order of the world, its λόγος, to Timaeus's fabulous tale, μῦθος.

When the demiurge represents the world in the image of the ideal gods, this representation is both perfect and imperfect: perfect in the sense that the world is the best of all possible worlds, imperfect in that this image will never, at any point or time, measure up to the model of the Ideas. The demiurge's power would thus be limited to the temporary instance of his own intervention, even if temporally indefinite. The world would be perfect, its order numerically constituted and its harmony ideally realized, *as long as* the demiurge would have the power to represent it all in the image of the Ideas. The demiurge's powerlessness would consist precisely in not being able to *definitively* inscribe the ideal principle of the world's conservation within its elementary genesis. The world's autarky would be purely mimetic, thus irreducibly dependent upon the demiurge's productive or poietic powerlessness. We will thus formulate our argument on the basis of the hypothesis according to which the image of the world involves a dual representation, each of these representations involving a specific time. On the one hand is the *demiurgic* or *noetic representation* of the world; this would be the conceptualization of the entire Universe and the production of cosmic time (between the motion of the planets and their numerical description). And on the other hand is the *genetic representation* of the world; this is the formation of the elementary becoming of the Universe and the development of a time of pure consummation, a time "preliminary" to any sensible organization of the world and "anterior" to any regular or successive order of the planets. This concept of time will determine an

---

4. We ought to note Proclus's attempt in his commentary to identify the entirety of Timaeus's account with the figure of the demiurge: "It's because the father of the *words* (πατέρα τῶν λόγων) should have a position analogous to the father of the *deeds* (ἀνάλογον . . . τῷ πατρὶ τῶν ἔργων) (41*a*)—because this cosmic creation [cosmopoiia] according to word (κατὰ λόγον) is an image (εἰκών) of the cosmic creation [cosmopoiia] according to intellect (κατὰ νοῦν)." Proclus, *Commentary on Plato's Timaeus, Volume I, Book I: Proclus on the Socratic State and Atlantis*, ed. and trans. Harold Tarrant (Cambridge: Cambridge University Press, 2007), 102.

irreversible loss, an irreducible expenditure of energy from which the world in its totality would silently suffer.

According to the conflictual reciprocity of these two representations, the demiurge's productive act would constitute both an act of the highest perfection, an act of idealization, and an unsurpassable state of powerlessness; that is to say that the world could be defined as the noetic representation of an Idea just as well as it could be thought as the representation of the demiurge's potential limits. It will involve both the perfect life of the immortal gods and the demiurge's symbolic death, his inoperativity. The world would thus contain the demiurge's poietico-mimetic limits within itself. But these invisible, intangible, indeed non-representable limits do not constitute a microscopic limit or macroscopic extremity but the absolute, that is to say irreducible imminence of a risk of decomposition, dissolution, and annihilation. The genetic order of the world would silently suffer from the possibility that the demiurge would no longer be the demiurge, that he become inoperative in his powerlessness to forever guarantee the ideal representation of the world.

Furthermore, in bearing the demiurge's mimetic paradox at the heart of its genesis, the world in its totality will never be reducible to a simple copy, a faithful double of the Ideas. In the ideal impossibility that paradoxically represents its greatest perfection, the world would at once become the sensible image (εἰκών) of the gods and an object of worship (ἄγαλμα) offered to the memory of their immortality. The world, in the universality of its totality, would have been mimetically produced as a votive object, an object henceforth destined to offering, gift, and sacrifice. This is what we will call the *tomb of the artisan god*. The world as image would be a sanctuary, a sacred temple, where the ideality of the divine is contemplated at the same time as the demiurge's announced death is indefinitely commemorated. There would no longer be any radical difference between the paradoxical image of the world, the simultaneous order between its ideal life and the threat of its imminent death, and the demiurge's state of survival, the irreducibility of his inoperativity. The world as sanctuary, the world as the starry heavens, will have been nothing else, in its confused mixture of ideality and flesh, than the momentary actuality of a survival.

Three movements will determine the inoperative state of this survival. Each of them will successively cut apart the text of the *Timaeus* in its most linear course. At stake are three types of demiurgic fabrication: a (material) *production*, a *representation*, and a *promise*. *Material production* (ποίησις) (28c) would consist of building a sensible order of the world on the basis of the four elements, or elementary corpuscles, given by the force of a primordial necessity. This movement will determine a proportional relation between each of the elementary transformations of the sensible world. And this law of proportion, defined in 32b, will constitute a self-regulating principle capable of maintaining the equilibrium of the cosmos between its losses and excesses. However, this state of equilibrium and conservation will only last for a time. And so long that the order of the world will remain dependent upon the dynamic principle of its constitution alone, its sensible body will be doomed to a slow but certain death.

To compensate for this state of rapid dissolution, and thus to suspend the potential limits of his productive act, the demiurge will now develop a *mimetic* (μίμεσις) *operation* (37d). It will be a matter of representing the sensible order of the world in the image of the Ideas, or the ideal model of the gods. In the demiurge's (self-) representation of the world in this image, he will insert an intelligent soul into this sensible body, and then the noetic principle of the Ideas into this soul. And the world will become the starry heavens: an organized heavens, proportionally here too, between the sphere of the fixed stars (the order of the same) and the revolution of the planets (the order of the other). While this noetic representation maintains the dynamism of the world in the constancy of an actual state of equilibrium, this order will only last the time of a representation. In itself, in its elementary structure, the world will always remain subject to the irreversible laws of dissolution. And the primordial question will become: for how long will the demiurge manage to represent the world to himself as the starry heavens? For lack of being able to ensure the world a genetic conservational autonomy, the demiurge must now commit his word; he will *promise* the world to never break the bonds that mimetically order it to the ideality of the model.

This last movement, this movement of the *promise* developed from 41*b* on, will constitute just as much a salutary act as the demiurge's most radical inoperativity. And here another paradox emerges. All the while committing his word toward the world, the demiurge will withdraw his productive functions and any responsibility that would bind him to the world. He will delegate his demiurgic power either to the subaltern gods or the divine heavenly bodies he just produced. Then, he will impose upon these gods the task of assembling, in the world as the starry heavens, a sublunary world that is not represented in the image of the Ideas, a world abandoned to the linear becoming of consummation. It will be a matter of sacrificing a part of the whole to save the whole, to maintain the demiurge's will in a state of goodness, and thus to ensure the ultimate commitment of his promises. The sublunary world, in the privileged figure of the animal, the human, and the philosopher, will be endowed with a very specific function: to make of its irreducible death the guarantee that the demiurge is ready to keep his promises. Insofar as he or she is a mortal being, the human philosopher must take on the demiurge's cosmic responsibilities. He must momentarily, in the time of his dying, take the demiurge's place and replace it with the thematic order of the concept.

In forming perfect concepts, in defining the ideal structure of the model of the Ideas in the purest of approximations, the Platonic philosopher will have combined the epistemic power of his soul with the ideality of his object; he will thus have liberated his soul from the organic ties that bind him to his body, such that, in dying, he will return to the world the perfect knowledge of its own-most origin. He will *give reason* for [rendra raison à] the reason of the world in sheltering its rational order from the likelinesses of his own account. According to the *Phaedo*, to philosophize is to learn to die. It is thus to learn to return to the world this ideality that the demiurge will never be able to definitively inscribe within its sensible body. For the human, by virtue of being a philosopher, dying will come down to—in the place of the demiurge— keeping the promise to never break the harmonious bonds that govern the world. This learning of death will thus produce a troubling alternative; it will be a matter of both avoiding the worst and playing with the worst. To philosophize is to constitute oneself as the living witness of this irreducible imminence: that the inoperativity of the demiurge be radical and without return, and therefore that the worst happens, that the possibility of the worst be actual, thinkable, and conceivable. From this comes the inevitable recourse and unexpected appeal to the philosopher's wisdom, his prudence, knowledge, and discerning power.

The world would thus have been endowed with a double model: that of a body in the imminence of its death[5] (this is the internal and necessary principle of consummation) and that of the philosophical elaboration of the concept (this is the external and contingent principle of idealization). Just as, in order to save the world from dissolution and preserve the demiurge's mimetic power, the philosopher will have to consider the world in the ideality of its principle, so too will the world have to be organized, in its genesis, according to the potential knowledge of this idealization. The sanctuary world, now become the tomb of the artisan god, will henceforth be indiscernibly combined with and inevitably suspended between the irreversible order of the cosmos and the epistemic power of the concept.

---

5. The thesis according to which the cosmological structure of the world in the *Timaeus* is built on the model of a living body has been developed by Rémi Brague in "The Body of the Speech: A New Hypothesis on the Compositional Structure of Timaeus' Monologue," in *Platonic Investigations*, ed. Dominic J. O'Meara (Washington, D.C.: Catholic University of America Press, 1985), 55–83.

Part I

The Cosmological Formation of Time

The Demiurge's Power

Birth of an Organization

The Implementation of the World: Classification and Hierarchy

§1. The demiurge is a polymorphous being, a being whose forms are of a great variety and an extreme complexity. Not only is it up to him to *judge* and *evaluate* what seems good for the best of worlds, but the art of *building* and *producing* the soul and body of the world in its totality also falls upon him. The demiurge's *power* nonetheless appears limited. It is restricted to the space and time of its own operation: to space, for the site where the primary elements composing the world are formed and assembled delimits a preliminary constitutive structure, to which each of the demiurge's gestures are absolutely subject; and to time, for this artisan god will only be able to produce a systematic assemblage of the world in accordance with a determinate order of succession and a rigorously enumerable duration. In fact, and in the strict sense, the demiurge is not an engineering creator but rather a divine architect. He has the supreme power in his hands not to produce the world from nothing but to survey, situate, construct, and realize the life of an organized whole from elements already charged or informed with radiant energy.[1]

---

1. Although the demiurge is endowed with very different figures, his power will be limited to the functions of an architect and his laborer. Plato will also attribute him rational qualities—he is a being of intellect (νοῦς) (48*a*)—and technical qualities—he is a craftsman (ποιητής) (28*b*). On the one hand, the demiurge

The Demiurge's Power

These forms of elementary energies, these δυνάμεις ἰσχυρὰς,[2] would for the demiurge constitute a necessary preliminary given, something like a regulatory source of continuous transformation (the chemical structure of the first assemblages of sensible matter), just as much as they would a chaotic source of gradual dissolution (the physical structure of an irreversible movement

reasons, he reflects (λογισάμενος) (30b, 34a, 55a), he believes (νομίζειν) (33b), he foresees (πρόνοια) (30c, 73a), he wills (βουληθείς) (30a, 41b), he consents (ἐθέλωσις) (41a), he speaks (λέγει) (41a, 41d, 41e), he even experiences emotions (37c). But on the other hand, insofar as he is the father who begets (37a), the demiurge will become a laborer, an artisan with multiple functions, such as a carpenter (28e, 33a, 36e), potter, surveyor, geometer, etc. (cf. Brisson, Introduction, 20–23, and, on the poietic question of building, by the same author, Platon, les mots et les mythes [Paris: La Découverte, 1982], 50–53; and finally Henri Joly, Le renversement platonicien: Logos, épistémè, polis [Paris: Vrin, 1974], 226–27). Originally, the term δημιουργός allegedly constituted a hypostasized form of δήμια ἔργα, from the substantive δῆμος, the public space, the land inhabited by a community, and the verb ἐργάζομαι (I work, I fashion, I operate, I labor). Its most proper sense would thus be something like "public laborer" ["travailleur public"] (cf. F. Bader, Les composés grecs du type de démiourgos [Paris: Klincksieck, 1965], 133–41). One therefore ought not confuse the demiurge's activity with that of the pyturge (φυτουργός) [maker] spoken of in book X of the Republic. In the famous hierarchical triad of the beds—the idea of the bed, the wooden bed, and the bed represented in painting—the pyturge would have created the ideal essence or the nature of the bed (μίαν φύσει αὐτὴν ἔφυσεν) (597d); it is thus a natural creator of paradigms. The demiurge, for his part, would have produced or built (δημιουργεῖ) a bed in particular, following the order of an appropriate artisanal technique and at the same time fixing his gaze on the model invented by the pyturge. "Surely no craftsman makes the form itself [τήν γε ἰδέαν αὐτὴν δημιουργεῖ οὐδεὶς τῶν δημιουργῶν]" (596c; PCW, 1200) (cf. Léonce Paquet, Platon: La médiation du regard: Essai d'interprétation [Leiden: Brill, 1973], 56–58 n. 5). Of course, the demiurge will represent a sort of anthropological analogon of the Ideas (cf. K. F. Doherty, "The Demiurge and the God in Plato," The New Scholasticum 35 [1967]: 517; and J. C. Nilles, "Approches mythiques du bien, du phythourgos et du demiurge," Revue Internationale de Philosophie 40 [1986]: 132–39), but his productive act will nonetheless never merge its product with the ideality of the model. This is precisely why the world organized by the demiurge in the Timaeus will never be similar (ὅμοιος) to the Ideas (30d), but close (παραπλήσιος) to the Ideas (29e). One already finds this distinction between the close and the similar in Diogenes of Apollonia's Fragment 9 (cf. André Laks, Diogène d'Appolonie: La dernière cosmologie présocratique, Édition, traduction et commentaire des fragments et témoignages [Lille, 1983], 46). One could further compare the demiurge's causal function described in Timaeus, 28a (cf. Philebus, 27b and 26e, 28c, 28d, 30d), which produces the proportional organization of the world, and the causal operation of immortal divinity (ἣ θεοῦ δημιουργοῦντος) described in the

of expenditure). This source of energy, of which the world is full from the smallest elementary particle to the outermost sphere of the fixed stars, would not be inexhaustible. And it is not for nothing that it was necessary not only to arrange an *order of the world* but especially to organize it in such a way that it would be assembled as *the only and the best of worlds*.[3] If the world must be unique

Sophist, 265*b-c*, which produces the animal and vegetal species of the world. On this subject, see Rémi Brague, "La cosmologie finale du *Sophiste*," in *Études sur le* Sophiste, ed. Pierre Aubenque and Michel Narcy (Napoli: Bibliopolis, 1991), 271–72 and 279. Regarding specifically the demiurgic cause described in the *Timaeus*, his designation as the Father of all things (τὸν ποιητὴν καὶ πατέρα τοῦδε τοῦ παντός) (28*c*) (cf. the ὁ γεννήσας πατήρ in 37*c*), one would again have to refer to the myth in the *Statesman*, where the demiurge is already defined by the figure of the Father (τοῦ δημιουργοῦ καὶ πατρός) (273*b*, see also 269*d* and 270*a*). Cf. Karl Reinhardt, *Platons Mythen* (Bonn: F. Cohen, 1927), 120 and 123, and Perceval Frutiger, *Les mythes de Platon* (Paris: Alcan, 1930), 204.

2. *Timaeus*, 33*a*. The δύναμεις would not constitute a mere formal potentiality (cf. Archer-Hind, *The* Timaeus *of Plato*, 100 n. 4). It would rather be a matter, as Cornford puts it, of a property that each body possesses, a capacity, a power to act or suffer (δύναμις τοῦ ποιεῖν καὶ πάσχειν). *Plato's Cosmology*, 53 (cf. J. Souilhé, *Étude sur le terme de ΔΥΝΑΜΙΣ dans les dialogues de Platon* [Paris: Alcan, 1919], 124).

3. The world is the most beautiful (κάλλιστον) work (ἔργον) and the best (ἄριστον) one (30*b*); it is moreover a single (ἕνα) work (31*a*): as it is born, so it will continue to be (γεγονὼς ἔστιν καὶ ἔτ᾽ ἔσται) (31*b*) (see the γεγονώς τε καὶ ὢν καὶ ἐσόμενος in 38*c*). However, how should we understand the ideality of this idea if, on the one hand, its model contains the totality of all intelligible living things (the νοητὰ ζῷα) (31*a*) and if, on the other hand, the world is the one and only representation that can correspond to this idea? According to book X of the *Republic*, the model will be defined as "a single form in connection with each of the many things to which we apply the same name [εἶδος γάρ πού τι ἕν ἕκαστον εἰώθαμεν τίθησθαι περὶ ἕκαστα τὰ πολλά, οἷς ταὐτὸν ὄνομα ἐπιφέρομεν]" (596*a*; PCW, 1200); on the *eidos* as "pure and by itself" (PCW, 57) see *Phaedo*, 66*a*, 78*b*, 79*b*; *Symposium*, 211*b*, 211*c*; *Republic*, IV, 445*c*, V, 476*a*, VI, 507*b*; and *Philebus*, 59*c* (cf. Victor Goldschmidt, *Le paradigme dans la dialectique platonicienne* [Paris: Vrin, 1947, 1985], 73). Each idea will involve a set of the world's objects, a set of representations corresponding to each possible thought of these objects. But only a real, single world can correspond to the *eidos* of the world as such (cf. Archer-Hind, *The* Timaeus *of Plato*, 94 n. 10; see also Jean-Claude Fraisse, "L'unicité du monde dans le *Timée* de Platon," *Revue Philosophique de la France et de l'Étranger* 172, no. 2 [1982]: 252); it is the world as the demiurge's mind represents it to himself. Likewise, in the *Parmenides* (132*d*), the hypothesis of a plurality of worlds would *ipso facto* involve a multiplicity of models of sensible worlds for any intelligible whole, a multiplicity analogous to the variety of forms

13

and perfect, and if it must consequently infinitely be produced up to the final stage of its completion and its pure idea, it is ultimately because the source from which it powers itself constitutes a limited and finite energy. Where, then, must one go in space and time to complete the world, and how many times will the demiurge have to improve his undertaking to infinitely recover the irreducible losses of its own expenditure?

§2. In the prologue to his account of creation (27d–29d), Timaeus puts forth the teleological principles of the organization of the world. According to his premises, order in sensible nature would always be the effect of a final cause (ὑπ'αἰτίου) (28a), to which each of the material causes will necessarily be subject; and this so as to *attain* a certain perfection—an ideal unity always identical to itself—and to *realize*, in the time it takes to accomplish this, the most stable possible functioning. In this way, each time he produces the world, and so long as he establishes its successive organizations, the demiurge, his gaze incessantly fixed upon what is identical (πρὸς τὸ κατὰ ταὐτὰ ἔχον βλέπων ἀεί) (28a), will have to make use of the ideal model of eternal being (or, more specifically, as we will see, *omnitemporal* being) (τὸ ὂν ἀεί): a being that is not born, and which only intellect (νοῦς) and reason (λόγος) can rigorously apprehend.

This radical opposition between an intelligible world (a model: παράδειγμα) and a sensible world (an image or a copy: εἰκών), once mediated by a teleological productive principle, a principle that tries to *persuade* material necessity to harmoniously organize itself,[4] will become incompatible with the reversible representation of the ancient Presocratic cosmologies with their indefinite cycles.

---

produced by the existence of a single paradigm (cf. Charles Mugler, *La physique de Platon* [Paris: Klincksieck, 1960], 8). See also *Timaeus*, 55c-d, where Plato puts forth the hypothesis of a plurality of worlds limited to five Universes (cf. Taylor, *A Commentary on Plato's* Timaeus, 377–79, and Richard D. Mohr, *The Platonic Cosmology* [Leiden: Brill, 1985], 12 et seq.).

4. "Intellect prevailed over necessity (νοῦ δὲ ἀνάγκης ἄρχοντος), by persuading (πείθειν) it to direct most of the things that come to be toward what is best" (48a; PCW, 1250) (cf. Anne F. Ashbaugh, *Plato's Theory of Explanation: A Study of the Cosmological Account in the* Timaeus [New York: SUNY Press, 1988], 31). Plato will have developed two concepts of persuasion, one dangerous and

It would indeed be absurd to posit a qualitative and gradual difference between two distinct states or moments of a single revolution for such universes.[5] It is necessary—for the organization of the world to be defined as a teleologically operating production, efficient and especially edifying—that the Universe where this world should grow be bordered by a stable and structurally delimited contour; this is the καθεστηκυῖα ἕξις spoken of in book X of *Laws*.[6] The Platonic world, structured in its principle by a rigorously proportional law is henceforth given over to a linear flux and to the successive progressions of becoming. It can therefore only realize

---

harmful, that of rhetoric (*Gorgias* 454d–455c; *Phaedrus* 260a; and *Theaetetus* 200e–201c), used by the Sophists to deceive their audience, and a learned, necessary persuasion. It is the latter to which not only the demiurge must have recourse in his building of the world but also the sage, in order to inculcate a noble falsehood to the rulers of the guardians of the ideal city-state: a falsehood (ψεῦδος) or a fable (μῦθος) capable of making them believe in the natural superiority of their birth and education (*Republic*, III, 414a-c, 415d; on this good persuasion, see also the *Statesman*, 304c-d, and *Laws*, II, 663d–664b).

5. Cf. Mugler, *La physique de Platon*, 16–20.

6. *Laws*, X, 893e. This constitutive base structure represents, on the theoretical plane, the two main dimensions of the *aurea catena Homeri*, the golden chain (σειρὴ χρυσείν) Homer speaks of at the beginning of book VIII (17–27) of the *Iliad*. This golden rope must both bind and oppose gods and humans, each pulling the rope from their own side to test the strength of their adversary. From the first interpretations of Homer in the classical age to Michael Psellos and Eustathius of Thessalonica, in the eleventh and twelfth centuries, passing by Proclus's commentaries on the *Timaeus*, the *Alcibiades*, the *Cratylus*, and the *Republic*, and Macrobius's study on the *Dream of Scipio*, this allegory of the *aurea catena* will have taken a dual path, which one can in fact find in Plato's text. It will represent the order of the world on the basis of two different types of *relations*. One will be properly *cosmological*, it is the internal and reciprocal relation of the four elements, which ensures a relation of composition and harmony between the heavens and the Earth:

> And finally, to put the crown on my argument, I might bring in Homer's golden cord (τὴν χρυσῆν σειρὰν), and maintain that he means by this simply the sun; and is here explaining that so long as the revolution continues and the sun is in motion, all things are and are preserved (πάντα ἔστι καὶ σῴζεται), both in heaven and earth, but that if all this should be "bound fast," as it were, and come to a standstill, all things would be destroyed and, as the saying goes, the world would be turned upside down (πάντα χρήματ᾽ ἂν διαφθαρείη καὶ γένοιτ᾽ ἂν τὸ λεγόμενον ἄνω κάτω πάντα). (*Theaetetus*, 153c-d; PCW, 171)

15

On this passage, see Jules Labarbe, *L'Homère de Platon* (Liège: Faculté de Philosophie et lettres, 1949), 328–29. The other type of relation would be *psychological*. This one would ensure a relation of cooperation between the celestial order of the planets and the circular motion of the soul.

> Now when each of the bodies that were to cooperate in producing time had come into the movement prepared for carrying it and when, bound by bonds of soul (δεσμοῖς τε ἐμψύχοις), these bodies had been begotten with life and learned their assigned tasks, they began to revolve along the movement of the Different, which is oblique and which goes through the movement of the Same, by which it is also dominated. (*Timaeus*, 38e–39a; PCW, 1242)

One will find the formulation of this double relation, both cosmic and psychic, in Proclus's commentary.

> Now the end (*telos*) of proportion is the friendship (*philia*) of the cosmos through which it is preserved by itself through itself. All that partakes of the friendly seeks to preserve that to which it is friendly, but all that is alien turns away [from the object of its enmity] and does not even want it to exist at all. Now, the cosmos is friendly to itself on account of proportion and sympathy (δι' ἀναλογίας καὶ συμπαθείας), so it preserves itself (ἑαυτὸν ἄρα σῴζει). But it is also preserved by the creation, receiving from it an "unbreakable" protection. For this reason, the Theologian [Orpheus] calls the bond that comes from the Demiurge (τὸν ἀπὸ τοῦ δημιουργοῦ δεσμόν) "mighty" (κρατερὸν), as when Night is made to say to the Demiurge: ". . . when round them all a mighty bond you have strung (*Orph. Fr.* 166)." Proportion gives this friendship to the universe, connecting and including the powers of the kinds in it. But Universal Nature (ἡ ὅλη φύσις) also gives [this friendship], engendering sympathy and the harmony of opposites. But prior to this, Soul (ἡ ψυχή) [gives friendship], weaving a single life of the cosmos and bringing all the parts of the whole into a shared harmony (συμπάθειαν ἐμποιοῦσα καὶ ἁρμονίαν τῶν ἐναντίων). And even prior to this, Intellect (ὁ νοῦς) [brings about cosmic friendship], creating in it order, perfection and a single connection. And even prior to the intellectual essence, the single divinity of the universe (ἡ μία θεότης τοῦ παντὸς) and all the gods allotted to the cosmos are originative (*prokatarchesthai*) of the unification found in it. And even prior to the many, the One Demiurge. And this greatest and most perfect bond (τοῦτον δὲ τὸν μέγιστον καὶ τελεώτατον δεσμόν) which the father throws all around the cosmos is productive of friendship and of harmonious association between the things in it—"the bond of Love, heavy with fire" as the *Chaldean Oracles* say. (*Commentary on Plato's* Timaeus*, Volume III, Book 3, Part 1: Proclus on the World's Body*, ed. and trans. Dirk Baltzly [Cambridge: Cambridge University Press, 2007], 105–6)

On all such questions relative to Homer's golden chain, the reader will consult the work of Pierre Lévêque, *Aurea catena Homeri: Une étude sur l'allégorie grecque* (Paris: Les Belles Lettres, 1959).

the ultimate end toward which its deployment tends at the price of a continuous restitution and the permanent equilibrium of the energetic forces, sometimes excessive, sometimes insufficient, of which it is constituted through and through.

But this philosophically decisive passage, from the eternal return of the cyclical spheres to the linear becoming of the world and its unique trajectory, must not conceal that this world is itself structured according to a circular motion. Quite precisely, but we will return to this, the demiurge will divide its specific regions, the sphere of the fixed stars and the revolution of the planets, according to the laws of a circular motion, and the living bodies of the sublunary region according to the laws of the ten linear movements.[7] This circular motion will not constitute the first principle of the functioning of the Universe, but will already itself represent a finalized and perfectly assembled *product* in the ordered whole of this Universe. On the one hand, it will *compensate* for the energetic expenditures of matter, and on the other hand, it will *fulfill* the ideal model of the immortal gods to perfection.

§3. In order to fathom the nature of the Universe or the whole (περὶ φύσεως τοῦ παντός), writes Plato, it is necessary to begin

---

7. Plato will speak in book X of the *Laws* of the ten different motions: displacement from one place to another (φορά); division by shock (διάκρισις); arrangement by gathering (σύγκρισις); augmentation (αὔξησις); diminution (φθίσις;); generation (γένεσις); destruction (φθορά); indirect (violent) motion; and the self-motion of the soul (as principle) (893e–894e) (cf. M. Gueroult, "Le Xe livre des *Lois* et la dernière forme de la physique platonicienne," *Revue des Études Grecques* 73, no. 169 [1924]: 33–35). Each of these motions will be implicitly referred to the *primary structure* of the cosmos, defined in 32b in the *Timaeus*. These transformations will thus thus be subject to the rules that regulate the proportional equation between the different forms of the cosmos. Failing that, the smallest deviation would risk irremediably affecting its primary structure and provoking, in a finite time, the gradual transformation of the Universe into another. Whence the necessity for the platonic demiurge to postulate a purely quantitative force of restitution (ἀνταποδιδὸν) (79e), capable of regulating the energetic exchanges and regularly reestablishing the original equilibrium (cf. Mugler, *La physique de Platon*, 14). On the theory of motion in the *Timaeus* (57d–58c), the distinction between τὸ κινησόμενον and τὸ κινῆσον, circular (κυκλοτερής) motion and the regular revolution of the whole (ἡ τοῦ παντὸς περίοδος), see Wolfgang Scheffel, *Aspekte des platonischen Cosmologie: Untersuchungen zum Dialog "Timaios"* (Leiden: Brill, 1976), 82–90.

by considering the birth or genesis of the world (πρῶτον λέγειν ἀρχόμενον ἀπὸ τῆς τοῦ κόσμου γένεσεως), then to finish with the nature of the human (τελευτᾶν δὲ εἰς ἀνθρώπων φύσιν΄) (27*a*). Between this beginning and this end, of which the death of the human, let us already note, would determine the infinite completion of the demiurge's noetic projections, a certain number of (successive) gestures seems to impose itself. Each of these will constitute a gradual *improvement* and an increasingly perfect *application* of the model to its copy. First of all, (1) it will be a matter of noetically *fixating upon*—and relentlessly so—the ideal forms of the model (28*a*). Then (2) to *assemble* a sensible, visible, and tangible world in the image of this ideal model by inscribing—by way of participation—a divine intellect within the soul of the world and inscribing this soul within its sensible body (30*b*). After which it will be necessary to respectively and specifically (3) *arrange* the body of the world, from the microcosm to the macrocosm, with the help of the four *primordial elements* (earth, water, air, and fire) (32*b*) and (4) *structure* the governance of its soul by a *mixture* of specific identity and continuous alteration (35*a*) and at the same time by a rigorously circular *motion* (36*e*). Finally, (5) it will be a matter of *shaping the organism* of the sublunary living things, from the macromolecules of marrow and flesh (73*b*–74*e*) to the physiological cycles of respiration and the circulation of blood (77*a*–81*b*).

It is quite obvious that the successive sequence of these gestures presupposes a very complex concordance. Between the first four and the fifth, between the production of the world and the birth of the human, the demiurge will have delegated his work to the functionary gods he just produced and that are subordinate to him. This final act of perfecting, by direct transmission, will be as fatal as it is decisive, since it will introduce the irreducible horizon of death into the living tissue of the world: the death of the human as the demiurge's radical inoperativity.

The World: Its Body and Its Soul

§1. The body of the world would form an animate substance in resemblance to the living model, and in the image of the totality of

18

all intelligible living things (πάντα νοητὰ ζῷα) (31*a*), and this soul would be a driving force endowed with intelligence. However, let us reiterate, the demiurge will not have created the world through and through; it is on the contrary in drawing (παραλαβὼν) from the heart of a still amorphous mass of always already radiant (visible) energies that he was able, within the limits of the possible (κατὰ δύναμις), to arrange the world in the image of the Ideas (30*a*). The demiurge's productive force and organizing power would henceforth be "limited" to the energetic powers (δυνάμεις ἰσχυρὰς) of the preliminary elements originarily at his disposal in order to build the world.

This elementary composition, as mathematical, chemical, and geometrical as it is physical, would constitute a very complex assemblage. Let us attempt to sketch out and then problematize its structure. If it is true that the world represents an ordered whole endowed with a sensible substance, it is also necessary that its body be as *tangible* as it is *visible*. But, according to the laws of elementary physics, there would be no tangible body that would not involve some *solid*, and no solid can be produced without *earth* (γῆ). Moreover, the presence of *fire* (πῦρ) seems indispensable for any body to be visible. These two elements represent the two extremities of the world; the central terrestrial core and the ignitive radiance of the fixed stars. To arrange a stable ordered whole with the aid of these two elements would further presuppose not only that their combination be rigorously assembled, but also that their assemblage be equally spread out among all the points of its sphere. This dual requirement of equilibrium and stability will be ensured through a logical relation of proportion (ἀναλογία), within which a middle term (τὸ μέσον) is necessary; with respect to the passage concerning us (32*a-b*), the middle term will be purely *geometrical*. In this way, and by definition, what the first term is to the middle, the middle will be to the last, and inversely; thus the pattern: [(a-b) : (b-c) = a/c = b/c]. The middle term can thus just as well become the first as it can the last, and each of these extreme terms can respectively become the middle term; they take turns in playing the same function, and the perfect equilibrium of the relations will be fully assured. But this middle ground between *earth* and *fire* is not realized through a single mediation, but by

19

two: *air* (ἀήρ) and *water* (ὕδωρ). Thus, as fire is to water, air will be to water, and as air is to water, water will be to earth. The thickness of the two internal layers (air-water) will constitute the two proportional mediums between the thickness of the two external layers (fire-air and earth-water); which will give us the following pattern: [fire/air = air/water = water/earth].[8]

This fundamental equilibrium ought to have ensured a stable and steady foundation for the multiple motions and numerous qualitative varieties that fill the world, a sort of economy of pure conservation concerning the extension of its body just as much as its continuous duration. Indeed, Plato's ordered universe on the one hand assumes the form of a sphere divided into four concentric layers, superimposed according to the laws of weight relative to the specific forces of their corresponding element (fire, air, water, earth), each of these layers thereby constituting the natural site (τόπον ἴδιον) (57c) of the elements *according to* their respective distance from the center of the Earth (62b). And, on the other hand, this same equation guarantees not only the continuous— *daily, monthly* and *seasonal*—regularity of the planetary revolutions, each according to its respective speed and the trajectories of its own revolution, but further still the regularity of the global cycle of the sphere itself—this is the *Perfect Year* of the Universe— the eight planetary revolutions regularly reuniting on a single starting point (39d).

Thus ordered in the duration and space of its body, the world would be spherical and circular (σφαιροειδές . . . κυκλοτερὲς) (33b). There would be nothing beyond its geometrical figure,

---

8. Charles Mugler, "Les dimensions de l'univers platonicien d'après Timée 32 B," *Revue des Études Grecques* 66, no. 309 (1953): 59. See also Catherine Joubaud, *Le corps humain dans la philosophie platonicienne: Étude à partir du* Timée (Paris: Vrin, 1991), 42–45. While this configuration of the Universe in four elementary concentric layers stems directly from Empedocles's cosmology, the two can nonetheless be radically distinguished. With Empedocles, the stratification by concentric layering and the encircling between the realms of Love and Strife constitute a transitional form of the Universe (DK, *Frag. 9*, especially lines 8–13; see Charles Mugler, "Sur quelques fragments d'Empédocle," *Revue de Philologie* 3, no. 25 [1951]: 41 et seq.). In Plato's cosmology, on the contrary, this stratification represents the logical configuration of an actual state of equilibrium, a mathematical structure toward which the entire Universe is constantly led back.

nothing to see, nothing to hear, nothing to touch, nothing to eat or anything to eject. Nothing could enter or exit (Ἀπῄει τε γὰρ οὐδὲν οὐδὲ προσῄειν αὐτῷ πόθεν) (33c).[9] The world will provide its own nourishment in feeding itself from its own waste. Plato thereby defines an αὔταρκες ordered whole, with no outside, without horizon and without remainder: a mobile sphere that is autonomous in the geometrical structures of its form and the physical trajectories of its revolution. But, if such an autarky seems to maintain the equilibrium of the καθεστηκυῖα ἕξις of the world in its qualitative and quantitative totality, this is not so for the energetic structure of the radiant forces of which each of the primary elements— proportionally gathered by the demiurge—is composed. A certain *gap* will come about between the proportional, geometrically determinate structure of the elementary bodies of the world and the fundamental equation of the cosmic energies on the basis of which the sensible body of these elements mathematically (or schematically) develops. As small as it may be, this gap will remain an infinite and thus irreducible gap. It will represent—in the physical and sensible stability of the world—the irreversible movement of its genesis, its becoming, and its death.

§2. Before returning in more detail to the at once disastrous and salutary consequences of such a gap, let us—once again very briefly—examine the quantitative structure of the four elementary bodies (53c–55c). According to the laws of basic geometry, every sensible body requires a certain *depth*, it is thus a *solid* (βάθος) body. And every solid is constituted by at least four *surfaces* (ἐπίπεδοι); every surface limited by straight lines and every rectilinear surface composed of (primary) *triangles* (τρίγωνοι). The smallest elementary corpuscles (πρῶτα σώματα) (57c) that constitute such triangles or nuclear particles would already comprise a *minimal schema*, and each of these corpuscles, by virtue of

---

9. One already finds this law of conservation in Anaximander; it is a law according to which the parts of the cosmos can become transformed without this modifying its totality (καὶ τὰ μὲν μέρη μεταβάλλειν, τὸ δὲ πᾶν ἀμετάβλητον εἶναι) (DK, *A1*; TEGP, *1*, 48–9). The same with Parmenides (DK, *Frag. 2* and *8*) and Empedocles (DK, *Frag. 8, 9, 11, 12, 13–16*).

21

the quantitative order and the rule of equation determining their assemblage, will delimit the qualitative figure of the elements in the form of a regular polyhedron.

Among the *primary triangles*, which all in principle contain a right angle and two acute angles, thus among those we call right-angle triangles, one will be *isosceles* (which "has at each of the other two vertices an equal part of a right angle" [53*d*; PCW, 1256], and which only has a single nature [54*a*]); another, *scalene* (which "has unequal parts of a right angle at its other two vertices, determined by the division of the right angle by unequal sides" [53*d*; PCW, 1256], and which for its part has an infinite variety of natures [54*a*]); and finally, the *equilateral* (a triangle formed from two scalene right-angle triangles). Two sorts of surfaces will emerge from these three primary triangles. The first will constitute an *equilateral triangle*, serving as a base for three types of solids. It will be composed, in all its perfection, of six scalene triangles (or three equilateral triangles), of which the length of the hypotenuse is the double of the smallest side. Two of these triangles will (laterally) combine to form the diagonal of a quadrilateral, and this assemblage will be repeated three times, such that the smallest sides of the right angles will meet and coincide in a single central point (54*c-d*). The second sort of surface will form the figure of the *square* and will comprise four isosceles triangles ("Arranged in sets of four whose right angles come together at the center, the isosceles triangle produced a single equilateral quadrangle [i.e., a square]" (55*b*; PCW, 1258).

From these two types of surfaces will finally emerge the *solids*, or *regular polyhedrons*. Among the four principal types (which correspond to the four elements of the world, respectively), the smallest, the lightest, determining the structure of fire, will be called a *regular tetrahedron*; it will comprise four equilateral triangles (or twenty-four scalene ones) connected by a 180-degree angle (54*e*–55*a*). The second will correspond to the element of air; this is the figure of the *regular octahedron*, formed of eight equilateral triangles (or forty-eight scalene ones), six vertices, and four 60-degree plane angles (55*a*). The third, the most complex, will represent the element of water; this is the *regular icosahedron* with twenty equilateral triangles (or one hundred and twenty scalene ones), and twelve vertices each formed from five 60-degree planes (55*a-b*). Last comes the *cube*. This fourth type of solid, determining the heaviest element, earth, differs essentially from the three other types of polyhedrons. The six square surfaces that comprise it—and which are opposed by their own vertices—are not formed of scalene or equilateral triangles as are the three other polyhedrons, but from (two) isosceles triangles (or twenty-four for the cube) (55*b-c*). This is why earth, as we will see, will not participate in the reciprocal transformations of the elements.

This quantitative assemblage of the elements expresses a nuclear structure of continuous regulation, a sort of *primary schema* determining the basic geometrical forms. Each of these schemas consequently organizes the continuous referral of these forms to their respective (numerical) properties. Without this referral, no proportion could guarantee the perfect relation and ideal distribution of the elements of the world among themselves; however, these basic forms and their various aspects will not be fixed once and for all. The *quantitative* transformation of the elementary corpuscles, their augmentation or diminution, will not be indefinitely realized through a simple restitution (ἀνταποδιδὸν) (cf 79*e*), neither immediately nor imminently. While these schemas may be quantitatively finite (according to the determinate number and specific structure of the primary triangles), the figural variety of their form will be qualitatively infinite. This infinite variety will produce an infinite number of combinations. From these combinations, an infinite complication of relations will be formed, thus creating a remarkable number of more or less large interstices (τὰ διάκενα) that will have to be immediately compensated for, and from this movement or this force of continuous replenishment will emerge an irremediable expenditure of energy.[10]

---

10. In Plato's physics there is no place for the void (cf. *Timaeus*, 58*b*, 78*b*, 79*c*). The general order of the cosmos must thus incessantly *compensate for* the interstices caused by the transformation and reconfiguration of the elements. It is from this force of restitution and instantaneous replenishment that every motion will find its source, and the world the origin of its irreducible expenditures of energy. On the Platonic question of the void (the κενὴν χώραν [58*b*], the κενότητα [58*b*], and the διάκενα [58*b*, 61*a*, 61*b*]), see Charles Mugler, "Le κενόν de Platon et le πάντα ὁμοῦ d'Anaxagore," *Revue des Études Grecques* 80, no. 79 (1967): 210–19; and Brisson, *Le même et l'autre dans la structure ontologique du Timée de Platon*, 397.

§3. Let us once again note that earth is excluded from any elementary transformation. As it becomes degraded or dissolves, no distinct element can be formed from its waste other than another piece of earth. Its geometrical form is a cube, and its mathematical schema is formed of isosceles triangles. However, between these triangles—infinitely dividable into smaller triangles of the same structure (square root of 2)—and scalene triangles (square root of 3) proper to the other elements, no type of triangle will be able to represent a form common to them;[11] because their reciprocal transformation is thus entirely *impossible*, this process will consequently be restricted to the three other elements.

As in Empedocles's cosmology, and contrary to Anaxagoras's and Heraclitus's theories, Plato's physics should presuppose two distinct sources of energy to explain the becoming of the world and its successive transformations. However, these two sources do not operate by taking turns, as do the principles of Love and Strife in Empedocles, but are produced *simultaneously*, and thus without involving the slightest gap of time between their reciprocal action. The first is a force of continuous *conservation*, whose quantitative ordering is absolutely subject to the mechanism of *necessity*. This is a movement that one must relate—before any noetic representation or taxonomic intervention of the soul (of the world)—to the schematic development of the nuclear particles (the triangles).[12]

This economic force of pure conservation has as its driving force the referral—without any interruption or the slightest delay—of each of the elements or regular polyhedrons to its specific

---

11. Cf. E. M. Bruins, "La chimie du *Timée*," *Revue de Métaphysique et de Morale* 56 (1951): 277.

12. There would thus be a certain logical anteriority from the dynamic structure of the polyhedrons to the cosmological order of the planets. The nuclear motion of the particles directly falls under necessity, while the rotational motion of the spheres exclusively depends on the noetic power of the soul. Cf. Léon Robin, "Études sur la signification et la place de la physique dans la philosophie de Platon," *Revue Philosophique* 86 (1918): 42, reprinted in *La pensée hellénique des origines à Épicure* (Paris: Presses Universitaires de France, 1967); Gueroult, "Le Xe livre des *Lois*," 40; and Mugler, *La physique de Platon*, 46 n. 1. As we will see below, to each of these orders will correspond a particular representation and a respective temporality.

site, a site that defines and delimits the concentric layer to which it belongs by nature. In fact, Plato writes, "as a result of the Receptacle's agitation (διὰ τὴν τῆς δεχομένης [*sc.* the χώρα; we will return to this]) the masses of each of the elements (τοῦ γένους ἑκάστου τὰ πλήθη) are separated from one another, with each occupying its own region (κατὰ τόπον ἴδιον)" (57*c*; PCW, 1260). This law attests to a strict quantitative equilibrium between likenesses. The other force, for its part, and radically opposed to the former, determines a continuous *alteration* of the elements. Cosmic equilibrium—this stability that ought to ensure the laws of homogeneity—is thus constantly disrupted, and the site proper to each of these bodies is no longer absolutely respected. This is why, each time an element enters into contact with another element of a different nature, and once it thereby modifies its basic schema, the latter element will be transformed according to the specific figure of the former and will tend to return to the proper site to which it will henceforth belong. Additionally, Plato writes, "because some parts of a particular element do from time to time become unlike their former selves (τὰ δὲ ἀνομοιούμενα ἑκάστοτε ἑαυτοῖς) and like the other elements, they are carried by the shaking (φέρεται διὰ τὸν σεισμὸν) towards the region occupied by whatever masses they are becoming like to" (57*c*; PCW, 1260). This law of heterogeneity between the similar and dissimilar is not opposed to the laws of homogeneity as disequilibrium to equilibrium but rather as *continuous* equilibrium to the *discontinuous* return of equilibrium.[13]

Each time an elementary body moves, whether in its proper site or in another layer of the sphere, each time it *modifies* the specific quality of its form (through the decreasing or increasing of its volume), or *transforms* the quantitative schema of its assemblage with respect to another schema, the *determinate number* of the primary particles or triangles composing each initial schema will remain identical and constant.[14] In any case of such a movement, the starting equilibrium appears assured until the end of the process, and

---

13. It will be a matter of substituting another force of restitution, another economy of conservation to the powerlessness of the cycles of continuous restitution, one no longer based upon the mechanical reinstatement of losses and excesses of energy but upon the eidetic laws of a purely regulatory idea.

14. Mugler, *La physique de Platon*, 216.

the totality of cosmic energy seems maintained in its purest autonomy. But the *simultaneous interaction* of these two forces becomes problematic. For if each of their respective motions were to become the sole master of the world, the annihilation of every sensible body up to the sphere itself would ensue after a certain amount of time. Pure homogeneity would create a static force of continuous rest (στάσις), and each of the concentric layers of the sphere would become fixed in place without a single element being able to cross its threshold; each of them would thus remain immobile, and the becoming of the world would be reduced to the forms of a pure illusion. Heterogeneity, for its part, would produce a state of gradual destruction (a sort of dissolution through systematic division) of the weakest elements (air and water) by the strongest (fire). And the entire Universe would constitute a great inferno filled with regular tetrahedrons.

§4. These two sources of energy will thus have to act in concert and thereby realize a single economic principle of conservation. It is difficult, however, to discern the exact axis of their interaction and determine the type of its inscription. Plato will nonetheless provide two reasons of principle. It will first be a matter of defining the general *cause* of a continuous heterogeneous force in the homogeneous medium of the sphere. It is *inequality* that causes the nature of non-uniformity, he writes (αἰτία δὲ ἀνισότης αὖ τῆς ἀνωμάλου φύσεως) (58*a*); it is a force that inserts foreign bodies into the layers where nothing resides besides polyhedrons of the same nature, different polyhedrons that spontaneously tend to return to their natural environment, thus creating a continuous displacement of energy. But what then is the *cause* of or the *reason* for the simultaneous inequality of the elementary corpuscles? Let us cite the text once more:

> Once the circumference of the universe has comprehended the [four] elements, then, because it is round and has a natural tendency to gather in upon itself (κυκλοτερὴς οὖσα καὶ πρὸς αὐτὴν πεφυκυῖα βούλεσθαι συνιέναι), it constricts them all (σφίγγει πάντα) and allows no empty space to be left over (καὶ κενὴν χώραν οὐδεμίαν ἐᾷ λείπεσθαι). (58*a-b*; PCW, 1260)

26

At stake is thus a centripetal force that, through gradual constriction, allows the fire tetrahedrons situated at the upper limit of the sphere to destroy a certain number of air octahedrons and water icosahedrons in decomposing their primary scheme through successive division. Thus, according to the principles of heterogeneity, these latter two elements, having become fire, and thus so many foreign bodies in their own environment will spontaneously tend to regain their new natural site (the upper zone of the sphere). The corpuscles of fire will direct themselves from the respective layers of air and water toward the region of the fixed stars, thus returning to the heavenly bodies the number of tetrahedrons they had to expend to maintain the centripetal force of their continuous radiance. From the quantitative schema of the elements to the successive revolutions of the sphere, the genesis and cycle of cosmic transmissions would be perfectly organized.

What follows from this double simultaneous force: *decomposition* (διάκρισις)–*recomposition* (σύγκρισις)? Will the cosmic becoming of the world thus be definitively sheltered from annihilation? From a quantitative point of view, the simultaneous operation of these two sources of energy will be able to momentarily reestablish the equilibrium between the radiance of the stars (the centripetal force of the sphere) and the production of tetrahedrons (the localizing force of matter). But in no case will it be able to compensate for the inherent losses of its own functioning. For this (simultaneous) operation itself takes time, and also requires a specific source of energy. This is a phenomenon of arche-originary erosion and dissolution of which Plato says almost nothing. Nonetheless, as Mugler notes,

> he realized that a part of the energy of the movement passed on to the particles of fire by the stars that threw them into the sublunary regions was absorbed therein by the very work of destruction it furnished (cf. 56*d* et seq.) and that these particles necessarily returned to their natural site, where the attraction of like by like brought them back after their journey, with less kinetic energy than they had brought with then upon departing.[15]

---

15. Mugler, *La physique de Platon*, 30.

The necessary and favorable conditions for the (genetic) production of motion, for the (chemical) movement of particles, for the (geometric) composition of the elements, and thus for the (physical) construction of the world would thereby constitute the very conditions of its own annihilation. Moreover, the double movement of decomposition by continuous division and recomposition by immediate movement will constitute what we will provisionally call the "primary time" of the cosmic restitution of the energies and of the irreversible becoming of the world. But how are we to understand such a movement and such a time before any specific organization of the Universe? This is what we must now attempt to analyze.

The Soul of the World and the Concept of Time

The World: Between the Heavens and the Soul

§1. The demiurge is a divine architect. His plans and his project, fed entirely by noetic aims, would impose upon him the supreme task of building or producing a world that would be perfectly suitable to the model of the Ideas, a world exempt from any aging, any sickness (ἀγήρων καὶ ἄνοσον) (33*a*), and pure from all dissolution. However, as we have just seen, in order to produce the world, the demiurge had to make use of a still amorphous mass of finite energies. The world indeed draws its potential source from a kinetic force, a sort of simultaneous motion between a centripetal and a centrifugal tendency, a whirling force that cannot indefinitely or generally restore more energy than it possesses. *In an indefinite time*, with respect to the energetic *quantum* it restitutes, this source is not in a position to add to or compensate for the equivalent sum of the expenditures that the simultaneous operation of its (force of) restitution requires of it. Something fallen and irremediably lost will always result from this world.

Here, in the finite state of the reservoir of potentiality that only the demiurge has at his direct disposal, the demiurge would find the *limits* of his productive operation. Plato is perfectly aware of these limits. Moreover, to shelter the world from its slow but gradual dispersion, and to thereby save (διασώζειν) not only the phenomena[16] but now the demiurge himself, as we will see, from the vain illusions from which his noetic operation risks suffering, it was necessary to grant him another productive power—a capacity, indeed a faculty that would allow him to assemble and determine the *perfection* of the world, the perfect circularity of its continuous motion, no longer (only) according to and on the basis of the elementary (mathematical, chemical, geometrical and physical) structures of its revolution, but according to the mimetic (psychic or phenomenological) representations of his construction. From properly *material* (laboring and artisanal) production (ποίησις) to specifically (reproductive or representative) *mimetic* production (μίμησις), the world will become an image. This image will be its soul (ψυχή); the form in which it will be seen in this image will constitute the illuminated vault of the heavens (οὐρανός), and this illuminated vault will represent a sort of sanctuary (ἄγαλμα) to the memory of the immortal gods.

§2. To save the world from dissolution, the demiurge, his gaze still fixed upon the model, had the genius idea to represent the world (to himself) as a figure harmoniously adorned with planets and fixed stars. He represented the world as a celestial vault—turning around the Earth—both *mobile* (according to the physical laws of the circular motion of the world) and *moving* (according to the chemical laws of the genetic motion of the elements).[17]

The representation of the world (or his world) as the starry heavens will properly fall upon the self-moving principle of the soul. However, this principle is both *dependent upon* and radically *separate from* the body of the world. The soul depends on it, since it too is a begotten (γεγομένη) being (37*a*) and, just like the body in its totality, it is partially made from a certain sensible substance (35*a*). But, on the other hand, it is thoroughly separate

---

16. *Timaeus* 22*d*, 56*a*, 68*d*. Cf. *Critias*, 114*d*; *Republic*, III, 395*b*, V, 460*a*; *Laws*, III, 687*a*, 677*b*; and *Letters*, VII, 332*b*.

17. Cf. Rémi Brague, *Du temps chez Platon et Aristote* (Paris: Presses Universitaires de France, 1982), 50.

29

from it. Contrary to the elements of the sensible world, the soul is endowed with intelligence and functions as the principle of its own motion.[18] Moreover, its formation is older (προτέραν καὶ πρεσβυτέραν) than the composition of the body (34c). One could also say, incidentally, that the soul is at once internal and external to the body of the world. On the one hand, the self-moving principle of the soul is wholly located within the body (it would be a matter of asking up to which elementary layer of the world— the geometric forms of the elements or even up to the primary scheme of their constitution—the soul can act and represent its body as the heavens),[19] and on the other hand the soul will border the smooth and external surface of the body. Plato writes, "in its center he set a soul (εἰς τὸ μέσον αὐτοῦ [sc. κόσμου] θεὶς), which he extended throughout the whole body (διὰ παντός τε ἔτεινειν) [and even beyond it (καὶ ἔτι ἔξωθεν)], and with which he then covered the body outside (τὸ σῶμα αὐτῇ περιεκάλυψεν)" (34b; PCW, 1238, translation modified) (cf. 36e) The self-moving force of the soul would thus constitute a sort of "interno-external" principle. It would thus be a being *outside* the world *in* the world.

Once the demiurge had the salutary idea of building the *soul* of the world, he implemented a triple operation: a *mixture*, a *proportion*, and an *orientation*. The first consisted in arranging a mixture from several successive mixtures. First of all, the demiurge made use of two distinct *substances* (οὐσίαι): one *indivisible* (ἀμέριστος),

---

18. While one often finds the idea of a birth of the soul in the *Laws* (X, 892a, 892c, 896d; XI, 967d), in the *Phaedrus* the soul is non-begotten (ἀγένητος) (245d). Is this the evolution of a thought or simply a contradiction? Cf. Raphael Demos, "Plato's Doctrine of the Psyche as Self-Motion," *Journal of the History of Philosophy* 6, no. 2 (1968): 133–45; and Brisson, *Le même et l'autre dans la structure ontologique du Timée de Platon*, 336–37. We will attempt to show that the soul in the *Timaeus* is begotten in the same way as time. Just as time, in fact, develops and is produced "in time," the soul will be produced *in ordering* the world in the image of the Ideas.

19. It is especially in book X of the *Laws* and in the *Epinomis* that, already at the nuclear level of the dynamic structures of the cosmos, the self-moving function of the soul will play the role of a regulatory principle (cf. Mugler, *La physique de Platon*, chap. 3). With respect to the relation between the *Timaeus* and the *Laws* (book X), the reader is invited to consult Gerard Naddaf's *L'origine et l'évolution du concept de physis* (Lewiston: Edwin Mellen Press, 1992) (cf. Frutiger, *Les mythes de Platon*, 201 et seq.).

always identical to itself (ἀεὶ κατὰ ταὐτὰ ἐχούσης), and therefore entirely intelligible; the other *divisible* (μέριστος), the sensible part that is begotten in bodies (περὶ τὰ σώματα γιγνομένης).

From these two substances, by way of a mixture (συνεκεράσατο) he formed a third sort of intermediary substance that would contain both a principle of identity, of the nature of the same (τῆς ταὐτοῦ φύσεως), and a principle of difference, of the nature of the other (τῆς τοῦ ἑτέρου). And from these three natures—the (intelligible) indivisible, the (sensible) divisible, and the intermediary substance (the same and the other)—"he took the three mixtures and mixed them together to make a [new] uniform mixture, forcing (συναρμόττων βίᾳ) the Different, which was hard to mix (δύσμεικτον), into conformity with the Same"-(35a; PCW, 1239).

He thus obtained a sort of harmonious mixture (μειγνὺς) from three distinct mixtures, a perfectly assembled combination, with the help of which he could now organize the circular motion of the world.[20]

At stake now is the demiurge's second intervention. The effectuation of this very complex action will be twofold: (a) Once the mixture is completed, the demiurge will divide the whole into seven parts—respectively corresponding to the seven planets turning around the Earth. This division will again be effectuated according to the laws of geometric proportion, having as its rule the reason of the *double* (1, 2, 4, 8) and the reason of the *triple* (3, 9, 27). Thus, in this division, the second portion will be the double of the first, the third the triple of the first and equal to one and a half times the second, the fourth the double of the second, the fifth the triple of the third, the sixth the double of the fourth, and finally the seventh the triple of the fifth. This gives us the following

---

20. In the *Timaeus* the concept of the mixture will return several times, notably when it will be a matter of describing the formation of colors on the basis of a mixture of tinctures and pigments (67c–68c). But it is especially in the *Philebus* that this concept will take on a decisive sense for Platonic ontology. The mixed genus will constitute both a mixture between *limited* and *unlimited* being (23d) and the *genesis* of their difference (25e). It is thus mixture that produces the genesis of the elements and engenders their opposition. Cf. Pierre-Maxime Schuhl, "ΓΕΝΕΣΙΣ et répétition: Philèbe 23c et suivantes," *Revue Philosophique de la France et de l'Étranger* 157 (1967): 120–21, and "Sur le mélange dans le *Philèbe*," *Revue des Études Grecques* 80, no. 379 (1967): 222–23.

numerical series: 1, 2, 3, 4, 8, 9, 27, corresponding to the respective spaces between the planets. Then (b), once this division is effectuated, the demiurge will take it upon himself to fill in the intervals (διαστήματα) subsisting between each of these portions with the help of two middle terms (μεσότητας). On the one hand, an *arithmetic* medium, for which the middle term "exceed[s] the first extreme by the same fraction of the extremes by which it was exceeded by the second" (36*a*; PCW, 1239), which will allow us to define the middle term as equal to half the product of the outer terms; thus, for the proportion 2 : 3 : 4, for example, we obtain 3 = (2 + 4) : 2. On the other hand, a *harmonic* medium, for which the middle term "exceed[s] the first extreme by a number equal to that by which it was exceeded by the second" (36*a*; PCW, 1239). Thus, in the proportion 3 : 4 : 6, for example, we obtain 4 = 3 + (3 : 3) and 6 = 4 + (6 : 3).[21] With the help of these two middle terms, arithmetic and harmonic, the demiurge will thus fulfill, among the intervals of the first division, both the series of doubles and the series of triples, thereby realizing an equilibrium that is just as stable, in its very principle, as the elementary composition of the sensible world.[22] However, the most important still remains to be defined. How was the demiurge able to produce from such a mixture a self-moving soul, a soul that in moving is capable of moving the world in the form of the starry heavens?

This third and last of the demiurge's acts is a very delicate operation, since it will be a matter of (c) *orienting* the world (36*c-d*). Three steps will thus be necessary. (α) Once the mixture is geometrically divided and harmoniously proportioned out in its smallest intervals, the demiurge will share it out into two parts (διπλῆν σχίσας), according to length (κατὰ μῆκος). After this he will cross these two bands in their center like an X, and then curve each of them in joining their extremities at the opposite point of their intersection. From these two concentric circles of tangible form and equal circumference, one will necessarily be outer (ἔξω)—it will form a smooth and indivisible figure; this one will represent the

---

21. Cf. Rivaud, Introduction, in *Timée-Critias*, 43. One will find this same idea of proportional progression in the *Epinomis*, 991*a*.

22. Joubaud, *Le corps humain*, 128.

substance of the same—and the other, inner (ἐντὸς)—it will form the primary series of the six geometrical divisions; this one will represent the substance of the other. These two circles will thus form something of an armillary sphere. Then (β) he will seize hold of (ἔλαβεν) this sphere and task it with a movement that always turns around the same point, always in the same way and in the same direction (καὶ τῇ κατὰ ταὐτὰ ἐν ταὐτῷ περιαγομένῃ κινήσει πέριξ αὐτὰς) (36c). With the demiurge's act of taking hold, each of the circles will not only be set into motion but, more precisely, *oriented*. The outer sphere of the same, more pure, will direct itself easterly from the left to the right, and the inner sphere of the other will displace itself westerly from the right to the left (36c).

Now that the distribution of the roles or functions is inscribed into the composition of the soul and that motion is thoroughly engaged therein, it is still necessary to (γ) define the relation between this (oriented) motion and each of its functions. The celestial vault will be born from this relation. Indeed, in the outer motion of the same there is only a single revolution, where the totality of the fixed stars are distributed out, while within the inner motion of the circle of the other, the seven (proportionally) entrenched geometrical portions of the mixture of the soul will constitute seven unequal circles for each of the seven planets turning around the Earth.[23] According to the series of the primary divisions, numerical proportion will express the respective distances of the planets from the space that separates the Moon from the Earth, namely: Moon 1, Sun 2, Mercury 3, Venus 4, Mars 8, Jupiter 9, and Saturn 27. This means, according to the harmonic rule of proportions, that three of the new unequal spheres will be strung together according to double intervals, and three others according to triple intervals; the seventh circle will correspond to the totality of the other circles (36d). In the circle of the same, the fixed stars will direct themselves from west to east at a uniform speed while, in the circle of the other—and while the respective movements of these circles,

---

23. On Platonic astrology, see among others Pierre Duhem, *Le système du monde: Histoire des doctrines cosmologiques de Platon à Copernic*, vol. 1 (Paris: Hermann, 1988), 51–85; Rivaud, Introduction, 52–59; and Wilbur R. Knorr, "Plato and Eudoxus on the Planetary Motions," *Journal for the History of Astronomy* 21, no. 4 (1990): 313–29.

as we will see, essentially co-imply one another—the wandering heavenly bodies will move from east to west according to different speeds. The three inner planets (Mercury, Venus, Sun) move at an equal speed. The three outer planets (Mars, Jupiter, Saturn) move at unequal speeds, in decreasing proportion with respect to how closely they approach the periphery of the fixed stars (36*d*).

We will return to this decisive distinction in more detail, as it directly concerns the question of time and the world as the image of omnitemporality. But for now, what do we know about the soul of the world? Plato in short describes it as a substantial mixture of the same and the other, a mixture that is logically and harmoniously structured in two concentric circles, whose respective trajectories are oriented according to the two opposed directions of circular motion. "Now while the body of the universe had come to be (γέγονεν) as a visible thing (σῶμα ὁρατὸν οὐρανοῦ), the soul was invisible (ἀόρατος). But even so, because it shares in reason (λογισμοῦ) and harmony (ἁρμονίας), the soul came to be as the most excellent of all the things begotten by him who is himself most excellent of all that is intelligible and eternal" (36*e*–37*a*; PCW, 1240). That being said, we know neither how the orientation of the sphere could have been born in its principle from the harmonious division of the mixture, nor how the sensible (supralunary) world could have become *figured* or *represented* as an illuminated heavens from this orientation. There is a very complex relation between the physical order of the world, the luminosity of the heavens and the harmony of the soul, a logical relation, bound on the one hand to the irreversible becoming of the elementary bodies (the irreducible expenditure of energy), and bound on the other hand to the ideality of the model of the Ideas (the immortal gods). We will attempt to define this relation on the basis of the concept of time.

The Two Concepts of Time

§1. After having successively organized the soul and the body of the world, and after having distributed this soul into the body, from its nuclear center to its outermost extremity, the demiurge made it so that the body of the world became the heavens and the heavens a mobile image of omnitemporality. The heavens are thus in a way an intermediary between the sensible world and the harmony of the soul, which, let us recall, itself constitutes an intermediary substance (a mixture), but a substance that for its part is situated between the world as the starry heavens and the ideal model of the gods. And, although the heavens are an intermediary being, their nature is nonetheless specific and, in a certain way, autonomous. They are an image (εἰκών), a copy, indeed a faithful double, according to the definition of the *Sophist*.[24] Furthermore, before

---

24. *Sophist* 236*a*. On the subject of this copy or double, one must distinguish two types of *mimesis*: εἰκαστική mimetics and φανταστική mimetics. According to the Visitor in the *Sophist*, representation will be *eikastic* or *iconic* if the symmetry of the model is reproduced (κατὰ τὰς τοῦ παραδείγματος συμμετρίας) (235*d*). Representation, by contrast, will be *phantastic* if the symmetry of a produced object—a statue, for example—is based upon the appearances or simulacra (φαντασίας) that come into view. The first mimetics will be described as a ἀληθὴς συμμετρία and will become the proper of philosophy. The second will be defined as a δοκοῦσα συμμετρία and will be reserved for the Sophist's activity; it is the art of producing a simulacrum (φάντασμα), an object that "appears the way the thing does but in fact isn't like it (φαίνεται μὲν, ἔοικε δέ οὔ)" (236*b*; PCW, 256) (see also *Phaedrus* 272*e*–273*b* and 260*a* as well as *Republic*, V, 476*d*, 477*e*, 478*a*) (cf. Maria Villela-Petit, "La question de l'image artistique dans le *Sophiste*," in *Études sur le* Sophiste, 74–86; and M. Lassigne, "L'imitation dans le *Sophiste*," in *Études sur le* Sophiste, 264–65). In a remarkably precise article, on the basis of certain fragments of Xenophanes's, André Rivier shows that, in sixth- and fifth-century texts (notably those of Herodotus, Anaxagoras, and Thucydides), terms like *eikazein* and *eikasia*, or *dokein* and *doxa*, or further still *phainein* and *phainomena*, do not in themselves imply any negative value, no form of illusion, vain fantasy, or error.

> For Xenophanes, as for his contemporaries, the objects of nature, beings and things, that fall under the senses, are not "phenomena" in the strict sense, because they are not "appearances." They are not there to manifest anything other than themselves; they exist solely for the function or usage to which they are destined. They are χρήματα. The world of "invisible" things, for its part, surrounds and penetrates the "visible"; it is constituted by "divine" forces that act upon beings and things, powers that make them live or die. More or less mysterious or familiar, proximate or distant, they exist as realities beside or among the objects revealed by the senses, composing or wedding themselves with them in the unity of φύσις. ("Remarques sur les *Fragments* 34 et 35 de Xénophane," *Revue de Philologie* 30, no. 1 [1956]: 59)

If the Parmenidean opposition between being and appearance had not already been established, it would have been impossible for Plato to found a general

asking *of what* exactly the heavens are a copy, let us attempt to determine *of what*, properly speaking, their imaged form consists. The demiurge's power, his noetic faculty, is a power of persuasion. It must convince necessity (that of the elementary structures) to submit itself to the harmonious laws of an organized world, so as to reduce *as much as possible* the infinite gap between sensible nature and intelligible nature. But why was it necessary that the demiurge, in his gradual labor of perfecting, have recourse to the acts of a properly mimetic production? From the primary assemblage of the elements of the sensible world to the harmonious mixture of the intermediary substances of the soul, it seemed the demiurge could only deploy a production of the material sort, a production whose product (here, the body and soul of the world) ought to remain directly bound to the productive acts of its composition, such that the world thus produced would remain indissoluble, in its global form, so long as the demiurge did not *will* (μὴ ἐθέλοντος) the breaking of its bonds (41*a*). "The realm of the world depends upon my willing (τῆς ἐμῆς βουλήσεως)," says the demiurge. This willing, which we will define below as a sort of promise, would indeed constitute a stronger and more powerful bond (μείζοντος ἔτι δεσμοῦ καὶ κυριωτέρου) than that by which the world was created on the day of its birth (41*b*).

The demiurge will have done his best. Indeed, according to what has just been said, the limits of his power would precisely correspond to the world's final state of perfection. He can of course carry on with the completion of the world, which he necessarily will do, as we will see, but everything he will have already composed will constitute for him, in this moment, the highest point of his art and knowledge. This is why, in any material act of production, the produced world will not only be limited—according

---

theory of imitation, where every image, appearance, and phenomenon would be entirely separate from the reality of the world and definitively thrown outside the axiomatic field of knowledge. And while the *Sophist*'s distinction between the icon and the phantasm appears strict, while it should in principle allow one to nuance or relativize the Parmenidean opposition, we will nonetheless see that, in the *Timaeus*, the iconic image of the world produced by the demiurge's mimetic activity can at any moment become reduced to the illusion of a phantasm. This is what we will below call the demiurge's transcendental illusion.

to the two senses of the term and without implying the slightest negative aspect—to the demiurge's laboring power, but will still depend on the deliberate actions of his own will. Everything thus leads us to believe that this will constitutes a power over the world—the unique and supreme power either to destroy or to conserve his own product. But, if the demiurge *can* will the dissolution of the bonds of the world, is this not the irrefutable material proof that the order he birthed will remain structurally dependent upon the elements composing it? Even if the world were harmoniously assembled, it would be fed by a force that devours or divides it from within, and which silently pushes it toward the irreversible becoming of expenditure. The world can shelter itself from this on the sole condition that the demiurge, during a still indefinite time, is capable of *representing* its order and harmony in the image of the Ideas. The will of the demiurge will thus be directly bound to the limits of his productive capacities. He will consequently have to call upon the acts of another force of production; precisely the one we call *mimetic*.

The material production and the mimetic production of the world will constitute the two poles of the demiurge's persuasive force.[25] But, differently from the first, the power of the mimetic is

---

25. "We said production (Ποιητικήν) was any capacity (πᾶσαν . . . δύναμιν) that causes things to come to be (αἰτία γίγνηται) that previously were not" (*Sophist*, 265b; PCW, 289) (cf. Brague, "La dernière cosmologie du *Sophiste*," 271). While Plato has at times associated ποίησις and μίμησις—for example, in the *Phaedrus*, 248e: ποιητικὸς ἢ τῶν περὶ μίμησιν τίς ἄλλος, and in the *Sophist*, 265b: Ἡ γάρ που μίμησις ποίησις τίς ἐστιν or in book X of the *Republic*, 606d: ὅτι τοιαῦτα ἡμᾶς ἡ ποιητικὴ μίμησις ἐργάζεται (cf. Hermann Koller, *Die Mimesis in der Antike: Nachahmung, Darstellung, Ausdruck* [Bern: A. Francke, 1954], 63–68, especially 67)—in the *Timaeus*, mimesis would have the function on the one hand of carrying out and perfecting the poietic fabrication of the world and, on the other hand, involve a constitutive relation between this world and the order of the Ideas, a relation of resemblance just as much as dissimilarity. As Jean-Pierre Vernant writes:

> With Plato, outside the cases where *mimeisthai* is used in the current sense, the accent on the contrary is quite decidedly placed upon the relation of the image to the thing of which it is the image, on the relation of resemblance that unites and yet distinguishes them. This explicit formulation of the relation of "semblance" that any type of imitation must realize brings to the front and center the problem of what, as much in themselves as in their relation to the other, the copy and the model are.

not limited to the demiurge's good will. One would be wrong in believing that the world is essentially distinguished from the Ideas by the sensible image he produces of them. The reason why the world, as perfect as it is, remains separate from the ideal model is not due to the fact it only constitutes its image. The image of the world does not only shape a copy in conformance with the Ideas, but first and foremost *represents* the demiurge's productive limits. Between, on the one hand, the idea he had to compose the world and, on the other, the idea to realize its image, we would have two radically different noetic acts. The first, while deliberate, is a *projective act*; a projection both dependent upon the finite elements at his disposal and subjected to the infinite perfecting of the ideal numbers. The second is a *reproductive act*, which no longer directly depends upon the demiurge's will. Of course, the god *willed* the production of an image. Not in the sense where he had the project and took the decision to make of such a product a being in conformance with the model, but in the sense that, at a precise moment of his projection, he imperatively *had to represent* the (potential) limits of his own production *to himself.*

Once the demiurge realizes this image, Plato does not say νοεῖ, as he does to designate the project of the creation of the world, but ἐπενόει (37*d*). The verb νοεῖν expresses the clear and precise idea of the mind's projections; it is to lucidly understand, it is to distinctively have the aim of a determinate object in mind. In this way, the noetic act will be directly linked to the intelligible content it apprehends. This is why it is perfectly suitable to describe the demiurge's gaze when he fixates upon the world of Ideas. The verb ἐπινόειν, for its part, does not, in the strict sense, express *what is*

The question thus openly posed is that of the nature of "resembling," of the essence of "semblance." ("Naissance d'images: Images et appartenances dans la théorie platonicienne de la 'Mimêsis,'" in *Religions, histoires, raisons* [Paris: Maspero, 1979], 108)

Aristotle, in his *Poetics*, will for his part establish a strict and univocal relation of dependency of the *poietic* upon the *mimetic*: "it is evident from the above that the poet must be more the poet of his plots than of his verses, inasmuch as he is a poet by virtue of the imitative element in his work (ὅσῳ ποιητὴς κατὰ τὴν μίμησίν ἐστι)" (9, 1451*b* 29–30; ACW, 2323) (cf. D. Babut, "Sur la notion d'imitation' dans les doctrines esthéthiques de la Grèce classique," *Revue des Études Grecques* 98, no. 465 [1985]: 77–79).

in the mind, but *what comes to* mind; it is what happens to it *after the fact*, whence the preposition ἐπι-.[26] It is a sort of "spontaneous" reflection *within* noetic projection itself. It thereby neither constitutes the act itself (the intelligent mind, the νοῦς), nor the aim of the act (the projective intention, the νόησις), nor even the targeted content of the act (the intelligible object or the model, the νόημα),[27] but solely this moment of internal reflection (ἐπίνοια) where the act itself represents to itself (through direct reproduction)—and without explicitly willing so—the relation between its specific *aim* and the determinate *content* of this aim. And this is precisely why, in the case concerning us at the moment, the representation of the world comes to the demiurge's mind: because it is *in projecting* the production of the world, and *in fixing* his thought upon the ideal model, that he *came to make himself an image of it*. This image thus was not first and foremost a degraded form of the model, nor even a conforming copy, but it determines the *reflexive relation* of representation that the demiurge's noetic aim (his νόησις) undertakes with respect to the intelligible content of its projection (its νόημα, or the ideality of the model). This image moreover constitutes the

---

26. It is interesting to note that the fourth-century A.D. controversy between Eunomius of Cyzicus and Basil of Caesarea, on the subject of the consubstantiality of Father and Son, essentially bears on the concept of ἐπίνοια. According to Eunomius, the term ἀγένητος (unbegotten) was the only name capable of expressing God's *ousia*. Any other predicate one could attribute to it would be but a pure conceptual invention (ἐπίνοιαι) (cf. Basile de Césarée, *Contre Eunome*, I, 22, ed. and trans. Bernard Sesboüé, with Georges-Matthieu de Durand and Louis Doutreleau [Paris: Les Éditions du Cerf, 1982–83]). Following Origen, who designated Christ's various aspects with the term ἐπίνοια, Basil responds to Eunomius "that it is not absurd that the Monogenic God receive different ἐπίνοιαι due to the alterity of the energies (τὰς ἑτερότητας τῶν ἐνεργειῶν) and certain analogies and proportions (ἀναλογίας καὶ σχέσεις)" (cited in J. Daniélou, "Eunome l'arien et l'exégèse néo-platonicienne du *Cratyle*," *Revue des Études Grecques* 69, no. 326 [1956]: 418). The preposition ἐπι- of the term ἐπίνοια, still quite close to the concept used by Plato, will have permitted, in a christological context, the establishment of a distinction that would ensure a sort of internal mediation, as temporal as it is ontological, between the eidetic intelligence of the Father (the νοῦς) and the carnal attributes of the body of the Son.

27. In the *Timaeus*, Plato speaks of the νοῦς in 17c, 26d, 27c, 29b, 30b, 34a, 36d, 37c, 39e, 46d-e, 47b, 47d-e, 48a, 51d-e, 68b, 71b, 77b, 89b, and 92c. For the νόησις, see 28a and 52a. However, there is no occurrence of νόημα (cf. *Meno*, 95e; *Symposium*, 197e; *Parmenides*, 132b-c; *Sophist*, 237a, 258d).

exact representation the demiurge makes to himself of his productive act, or more precisely, of the *relation*, indeed the *gap* between his projection and its ideal object.

If this hypothesis holds, the heavens would thus constitute the *demiurgic representation* of the world; they would determine the representation that the demiurge realizes in producing the world or, more precisely, in producing the soul and the harmony of the world.

The illuminated vault of the heavens will no longer be definable as a purely noetic project (a simple concept), nor be thought of as a strictly material product (a physical structure), but can only be described as a pure object of *mimesis*. It is a mimetic moment *in* the production of the world. With the concept of the heavens, we are in the presence of a determinate cosmological state: the momentary state of the world as the demiurge *had* to represent it to himself *as* he experienced the gap that separates the sensible from the intelligible. And this determinate moment will precisely constitute the cosmological limits of his own power. It will constitute the order of the world and at the same time open the world [*le monde*] onto the unfit or the unworldly [*l'immonde*], onto the state of the world that none of the demiurge's noetic projections could adequately represent.

§2. In the famous passage from the *Timaeus* where the concept of time would usually mean "a moving image of eternity" (37*c-d*; PCW, 1241), the distinction between the two noetic acts is rigorously upheld. We will translate this passage in its context, taking into account Brague's arguments that make of the subject of this image not time, but in fact the heavens.[28]

Now, when the father who had begotten (γεγονὸς) it saw and understood (ἐνόησεν) that it moved and lived (κινηθὲν αὐτὸ καὶ ζῶν), this world, a sort of shrine (ἄγαλμα) to the omnitemporal gods (τῶν ἀιδίων θεῶν), he was filled with admiration (ἠγάσθη), and, delighted by its charm (εὐφρανθεὶς), the idea came to his mind (ἐπενόησεν) of making it more like its model still (ἔτι δὴ μᾶλλον ὅμοιον πρὸς τὸ παράδειγμα). And, given that the model was itself an omnitemporal living thing, likewise (οὕτως) did he [the

---

28. Brague, *Du temps chez Platon et Aristote*, 43–71.

father] undertake (ἐπεχείρησε)—insofar as this was possible (εἰς δύναμιν)—bringing the whole to completion (ἀποτελεῖν) so that it too would have that nature (τοιοῦτον). Now, it was the living thing's [model's] nature ('Η μὲν οὖν τοῦ ζῴου φύσις) to be omnitemporal (αἰώνιος), and this nature (τοῦτο), to bestow it at every point and to the end (παντελῶς προσάπτειν) upon anything begotten is impossible (οὐκ ἦν δυνατόν). Also came to the demiurge's mind (δ'ἐπενόει) the idea of making a certain mobile image of omnitemporality (εἰκὼ . . . κινητόν τινα αἰῶνος ποιῆσαι) and, at the same time as he ordered the heavens (καὶ διακοσμῶν ἅμα οὐρανὸν), he would make [of it] an image of omnitemporality remaining in unity, an image moving according to omnitemporal number (ποιεῖ μένοντος αἰῶνος ἐν ἑνὶ κατ'ἀριθμὸν ἰοῦσαν αἰώνιον εἰκόνα). This very (τοῦτον) number we now call "time" (ὃν δὴ χρόνον ὠνομάκαμεν). (37c-d; cf. PCW, 1241, translation modified)

The two great innovations of this translation, which we owe to Brague,[29] would be on the one hand to have thought of the image of αἰών not as time but as the heavens, and on the other hand to have attributed the adjective αἰώνιον not to the image, that is to say to the heavens, but to the number according to which the heavens move; which would once again invalidate the traditional and, we will see, irrelevant *opposition* between time and αἰών. We will divide this passage into two parts. In the first (37c-d), the noetic distinction between the demiurge's understanding with respect to his work (the moving and living world) and the feeling he experiences *in* this understanding is explicit. Not only is the demiurge stunned and surprised by what he sees; he is also and most of all charmed to see the realization of the world produced of his own power. He is delighted by the idea of knowing up to what point his undertaking will have allowed him to reduce the infinite gap between the sensible world and its ideal model.

---

29. Brague proposes the following "explanatory translation":

> He had the idea of making a mobile image of the noetico-numerical content of the Living Thing [*du Vivant*]. He thus granted an ordered distribution to the whole of the heavenly bodies. In so doing, he built an image of this content. So while the content remains in its place, the heavens that are its image advance according to the number expressing this content, this number we call time. (*Du temps chez Platon et Aristote*, 61)

In closely following the text, one can say that, if the idea came to the demiurge to further perfect his work, of making it more similar to the model in defining it as an image, it is due to the delight that overtakes him at the sight (νόησις) of this work. It is this delight that *provoked within him* the idea of an improvement, and not the other way around. But what, in this context, does being delighted (εὐφράζειν) mean? Once the demiurge caught sight of his power, his heart or mind (φρήν) was delighted. His heart is thus taken, or more precisely "taken well." Which means, according to the strict sense of the adverb ἐυ, that it is taken at the right place, *where it must be,*[30] where and when, consequently, his productive power and ownmost authority are at their highest. However, it will not have escaped Plato to strongly emphasize that to perceive such a power is at the same time, for the demiurge, to experience something impossible: to realize the *perfect* application of the world to the ideal model. And it is in noting, we were saying, that at the highest point of his power, where it would always and forever remain impossible for him to complete his undertaking, the idea came to him to *represent* the world, in the image of this model, as the starry heavens.

But we must be even more precise and ask ourselves *at what moment* of his operation such an undertaking came to mind. The temporal order of the demiurge's divine gestures is very complex. On the one hand, the composition of the soul of the world must *precede* the building of its body, but on the other hand, the assembled whole of the soul must *presuppose* the existence of a sensible matter, since it is in part composed of the latter. Moreover, the heavens involve the presence of the soul of the world just as much as that of its body. Once Timaeus *prescribes* the principal rules of the world's composition, and does so "before" any direct and material involvement of the demiurge, the world must necessarily be conceived of in the image of something, a transcendent and absolute model (29*b*). But, can we read this prescription as a deliberate intention on the demiurge's part? No, of course, since the ultimate goal (τέλος) of his operation is not to produce the world

---

30. Cf. Pierre Chantraine, *Dictionnaire étymologique de la langue grecque* (Paris: Klincksieck, 1968), 388, 1.

as image but to reduce, *through the representation* of this world—
and as much as his power would allow—the gap between this still
amorphous mass of finite energies and the numerical forms of
the ideal model of the gods. One must thus admit that this idea of
representation is an idea *after the fact,* and that it could only have
intervened *at the very moment when,* the demiurge observing the
excellence of his product, he experienced the impossible harmony
between the highest point of his productive capacities (the world
as starry heavens) and the ultimate aim of these noetic projections
(the world of the ideal numbers).

This moment of representation nonetheless remains difficult
to grasp. According to the second part of the passage cited (37*d*),
not only does Plato describe a certain relation of consequence
between the impossible perfect application of the model to the
begotten body and the representation of its image—a relation ex-
pressed through the oppositional correlation μὲν . . . δέ (36*d*)—
but he further specifies that this image was produced at the same
time (ἅμα) as the heavens were ordered (36*d*). The ordering of the
heavens, as the circular movement of the planets and the fixed
stars, constitutes a very specific phase in the composition of the
world. It is the moment when the demiurge *distributes* the harmony of the soul of the world in the smallest parts of its sensible
body. One can thus say, as a matter of consequence, that it was *by
placing* and *by distributing* the soul into the body of the world—
and thereby observing that it was nevertheless impossible to fully
close the gap between the sensible and the intelligible—that he
represented this world to himself in the form of the heavens. We
will see below that this inscription of the soul into the body will
correspond—at the sublunary level of the human race—to a state
of madness, folly, and properly empirical illusion. For the demiurge, from the *impossibility* of closing this gap through such a harmony there will result both a representation of the world and the
implicit risk of making a specifically noetic (or demiurgic) illusion
of this world, an illusion of the transcendental type, which will
involve, as we will see, a double risk: that, on the one hand, the
world exists nowhere outside the demiurge's representation, such
that Timaeus's account would be nothing other than its fable, and
on the other hand that the demiurge be incapable to indefinitely

represent this world in the image of the Ideas. This is what we will below call the demiurge's symbolic death through the effective annihilation of the world. But, before coming to this ultimate point of mimetic production, as salutary as it is disastrous, let us ask ourselves, closely following the *Timaeus*, what serves to ground the concept of representation, and how, properly speaking, is this concept articulated?

§3. Still in the second part of the passage just cited, after having related the demiurge's potential limits to his representation of the world, Plato will describe such a relation as a genuine *temporal operation*. We will sketch it out in five points: (1) the image the demiurge represents in producing the heavens (that is to say in inserting the soul into the body of the world) must be a mobile image of omnitemporality; (2) this omnitemporality is defined as a being that always remains in unity; (3) the movement of this image of unity advances according to number; (4) this number too is omnitemporal; and (5) one designates this omnitemporal number through the concept of time. Let us now examine each of these points.

What does it mean for the heavens to be an image of omnitemporality? While the term οὐρανός has at times been conflated, in the *Timaeus*, with the notion of world (κόσμος), indeed with the whole itself (τὸ πᾶν)—both of which in principle include the terrestrial globe, while the heavens seem to exclude it[31]—in its strictest and most rigorous usage, "the heavens" designates the completed representation of both the *circular* and *visible* motion

---

31. There would thus be a strict difference between *ouranos* and *cosmos*. Contrarily to Anaximander's cosmology (*Frag.* 12 A 9; cf. Marcel Conche, *Anaximandre: Fragments et témoignages* [Paris: Presses Universitaires de France, 1991], 159–60), Plato's *cosmos* would be greater than *ouranos*. While *ouranos* would contain only the sphere of the planets and the fixed stars that turn around the Earth (*Timaeus*, 22d, 23d, 39d; cf. 90a and 91e), *cosmos* can at times come down to *ouranos* (28b), sometimes involving the Earth (52b), at times including the region that goes from the Earth to the Moon, and thereby coming down to the entire Universe (τὸ πᾶν) (27a and 47a) (cf. David Keyt, "The Mad Craftsman of the Timaeus," *Philosophical Review* 80, no. 2 [1971]: 233). Let us note that in other texts, the notion of world involves the heavens just as much as the Earth: *Gorgias*, 508a; *Euthydemus*, 296d; *Sophist*, 232c; *Philebus*, 28c.

of the world. They are the (mobile) totality of the heavenly bodies, wandering and fixed, that the soul will have harmoniously organized once inserted into the world. This global motion, first of all, constitutes the double cyclical motion of an armillary sphere. On the one hand, it constitutes the *motion of the other*; it determines in their totality the respective movements of the seven planets turning around the Earth, from east to west. On the other hand, it constitutes the *motion of the same*; it is this motion that both prescribes and regulates the equilibrium of the different periods proper to each of the planetary motions, and at the same time determines the single period of the motion of the fixed stars. Thus the motion of the heavens is all the more luminous. As Plato writes:

And so that there might be a conspicuous measure (μέτρον ἐναργές) of their relative slowness and quickness with which they move along in their eight revolutions, the god kindled a light (φῶς ὁ θεὸς ἀνῆψεν) in the orbit second from the earth, the light that we now call the Sun. Its chief work would be to shine upon the whole universe (ἵνα ὅτι μάλιστα εἰς ἅπαντα φαίνοι τὸν οὐρανὸν) and to bestow upon all those living things appropriately endowed and taught by the revolution of the Same and the uniform (μαθόντα παρὰ τῆς ταὐτοῦ καὶ ὁμοίου περιφορᾶς), a share in number (μετάσχοι τε ἀριθμοῦ). (39*b-c*; PCW, 1242)

The (solar) luminosity of celestial motion thus has another function, just as constitutive as its circularity.[32] Just as the *circularity* of the circle of the same participated in the ideal forms of the model, the *luminosity* of the circle of the other will allow one to discern and recognize the numerical form of the model. It is in fact from such a light that the daily cycles of day and night will be born, these cycles through whose (numerical) figure the world is shaped as a visible being. Thus to each planet will correspond a specific and numerically determinate period according to the trajectory of its orbit: we will speak of a month when the Moon catches up to the Sun and a year when the Sun completes its orbit. And even if no one will have ever named—or enumerated—the five other

---

32. *Timaeus*, 47*a-b*. Cf. Brague, *Du temps chez Platon et Aristote*, 59.

planets in such a manner, their respective movements will none-theless be assembled according to a *determinate order of time*. It will be so in the pure equilibrium of proportions and up to the perfect number of time (ὅ τέλος ἀριθμός χρόνον), namely the Perfect Year "at that moment when the relative speeds of all eight periods have been completed together and, measured by the circle of the Same that moves uniformly, have achieved their consum-mation" (39*d*; PCW, 1243).

Before coming back to the numerical function of these two re-ciprocal times, one can already see that the demiurge organizes the heavens as an image on the basis of a dual operation: on the one hand by harmoniously distributing each of the heavenly bodies along their respective orbits, all the while continuously maintain-ing this order in an *actual* state of equilibrium; on the other hand by providing the means for these heavenly bodies to visibly show the involvement between this harmony and the ideal numbers. In short, it is because the cycle of the planetary revolutions is *numer-ically determinate* that it can participate in the world of Ideas. The heavens are thus at once an *image*, since they noetically realize the representation of the world that the demiurge makes for himself; a *mobile* image, since they represent the perfect assemblage of circu-lar motion; and a mobile image of *omnitemporality* (αἰών), since, through the visible enumeration of their course, they let it be seen and understood that they participate of the omnitemporal Ideas.

But what exactly does the concept αἰών mean, and how do we justify its translation by "omnitemporality"? This term is difficult to define, first of all because it is forcefully and thoroughly assim-ilated to the intemporal forms of eternity, and next because Plato himself will have attributed it two distinct adjectives: αἰώνιος (ac-centuated, if one can say so, by διαιώνιος) and ἀΐδιος. The first, very rare in Plato, concerns the nature of the living model (37*d*, 38*b*, 39*e*) just as much as it does number itself (37*d*); the second will designate the living thing as such, in itself, without qualitative specification (37*b-c*, 37*d*, 40*b*).[33]

---

33. The adjective αἰώνιος, with the term κινήτος, would constitute the two attributes of αἰών (on this rare adjective, see the *Republic*, II, 363*d*, and *Laws*, X, 904*a*). The substantive ἀΐδιος, for its part, would be composed of the suffix -ίδιος, which generally serves to form derivations from adjectives or adverbs in the local

Let us recall first of all that the term αἰών did not originally express the infinite idea of a continuity, whether that of *aeternitas* (primary eternity) or that of *sempiternitas* (secondary eternity, *aevum*), but on the contrary designates the "age of a life" [*"l'âge d'une vie"*]. It is of course a matter of a *long* duration, but it is a *finite* duration.[34] We also find this use several times

or temporal sense (cf. Pierre Chantraine, *Formation des noms en grec ancien* [Paris: Klincksieck, 1933], 39). These terms would thus indicate something that can be found somewhere, or something that happens at a given moment. Consequently, ἀίδιος would designate what happens ἀεί, what occurs ἀεί, for a long time, over a long period of time, several days, indeed forever (cf. Conrad Lackeit, *Aion: Zeit und Ewigkeit in Sprache und Religion der Griechen, Erster Teil: Sprache* [Königsberg: Hartung, 1915], 56 et seq.; and Otto Weinreich, "Aion in Eleusis," *Archiv für Religionswissenschaft* 19 [1919]: 177 et seq.). This term, however, does not mean "what necessarily lasts forever," but that of which one can never say with assurance that it began here and now and that it will one day finish at such and such a point, whence the implicit risk of reducing its sense to the intemporal idea of an eternity. Incidentally, one will find in Plotinus, on the subject of the intelligible world, an assimilation between αἰώνιον and ἀίδιον. Cf. Plotinus, *Enneads: Volume III*, trans. A. H. Armstrong (London: William Heinemann LTD, 1980), 7: "On Eternity and Time," 3, lines 1–3, pages 302, 303. On these terms, and in the context of the *Timaeus*, see especially Brague, *Du temps chez Platon et Aristote*, 30 and 63–69; Hedwig Conrad-Martius, *Die Zeit* (München: Verlag Kösel, 1954), 95–97; Gernot Böhme, *Zeit und Zahl: Studien zur Zeittheorie bei Plato, Aristoteles, Leibniz und Kant* (Frankfurt am Main: Vittorio Klostermann, 1971), 68, 83, and 150; and Karen Gloy, *Studien zur Platonischen Naturphilosophie im* Timaios (Würzberg: Königshausen + Neumann, 1986), 56–57. The latter two authors, while translating these terms with *Äon* and *äonische*, will have nonetheless understood its sense on the basis of a traditional idea of supra-temporality (*Überzeitlichkeit*).

34. As Émile Benveniste writes, "while the expression 'eternity' is not yet fixed in its abstract specificity in Indo-European, it tends to realize itself through the words meaning 'age,' 'long duration' constituting the Indo-Iranian family *ayu-*, gr. αἰών, ἀεί, lat. *aevus, aeternitas*, got. *aiws*, etc." "Expressions indo-européennes de l'éternité," *Bulletin de la Société de Linguistique Française* 38 (1937): 103 (cf. André-Jean Festugière, "Sens Philosophique du mot ΑΙΩΝ: À propos d'Aristote, *De Caelo* I, 9," *Études de Philosophie Grecque* [Paris: Vrin, 1971], 255–57; R. B. Onians, *The Origins of European Thought: About the Body, the Mind, the Soul, the World, Time and Fate* [Cambridge: Cambridge University Press, 1991], 208–9; and Enzo Degani, *Aἰών: Da Omera ad Aristotele* [Padova, Cedam, 1961], 215 et seq.). Let us note that, in Anaximander's cosmology, αἰών constituted the cycle of an inexhaustible vital force, where the beginning and the end of a generation originarily met within the infinite. According to the testimony of Pseudo-Plutarch, Anaximander would have said that

the boundless [τοῦ ἀπείρου] contained the whole cause of coming to be and perishing of the world, from which [ἐξ οὗ] he says the heavens are separated and generally all the world-orders, which are countless. And he declared perishing to take place and much earlier coming to be, all these recurring (ἀνακυκλουμένων) from an infinite time past (ἐξ ἀπείρου αἰῶνος). (DK, *12 A 10*; TEGP, *19*, 56–57)

On this time of life, see also Empedocles, *Fragment 17*, as well as verses 899–900 of Euripides's *Heraclidae*, where it is said that "Fate that gives completion and Life, time's child bring many things to pass (πολλὰ γὰρ τίκτει Μοῖρα τελεσσιδώτειρ Αἰών τε Χρόνου παῖς)." Euripides, *Heraclidae*, trans. David Kovacs (Cambridge: Harvard University Press, 1995). Just as for Μοῖρα, there would be a personification of Αἰών. On the one hand, *aiōn* takes on the figure of destiny, as with the tragedians (see Sophocles, *Trachiniae*, 34, and Euripides, *Andromache*, 1214 et seq.), and, on the other hand, clearly through the influence of Aristotle, *aiōn* will be defined as the very figure of the Heavens; it is the *soul of the world* of which several writers of the late Hellenism will speak, notably Marcus Messala (cf. M. Zepf, "Der Gott Αἰών in der hellenischen Theologie," *Archiv für Religionswissenschaft* 25 [1927]: 225 et seq.). L. Couloubaritsis will have attempted to propose a distinction in Heraclitus's *Fragment 52* (TEGP, *154*, 179) (αἰών παῖς ἐστι παίζων πεσσεύων᾽ παιδὸς ἡ βασιληίη) between the notion of a time belonging to the constitutive elements of the world (especially *fire*) and Αἰών as the time of life proper to every thing. "La notion d'Aion chez Héraclite," in *Ionian Philosophy*, ed. K. J. Boudouris (Athens: Ionia Publications, 1989), 111 (cf. Ernesto Leibovich, "L'Aiôn et le temps dans le *Fragment B52* d'Héraclite," *Alter: Revue de Phénoménologie* 2 [1994]: especially 97–99). It is also interesting to note that Basil of Caesarea, again in his debate with Eunomius, will use the term αἰών as an intermediary form, an *interval* (διάστημα) between the eternity (ἀίδιος) proper to God the Father and the cosmic time (χρόνος) proper to the nature of the human. *Contre Eunome*, II, 13, 19–22 (cf. E. Owen, "αἰών and αἰώνιος," *Journal of Theological Studies* 37 [1963]: 271). The αἰῶνες that most of the Latin translations translated by *siècle* (*saecula*) at the time of Basil of Casearea (cf. Letter to the Hebrews 1, 2, and Letter to the Corinthians *I*, 1, 2, 3 ; 65, 2, as well as Pope Clement 1 [Letter to the Romans 20, 12; 32, 4; 35, 3; 38, 4; 43, 6; 45, 7; 50, 7; 55, 6; 58, 2]) will constitute the creatures of the Son (*Contre Eunome* II, 17, 40–41), distinct from the eternity of the Father (*Contre Eunome* II, 17, 56–57). (On αἰών as *siècle*, see Eunomius of Cyzicus's *Apology*, 10, 5. 10. 11; 27, 13; 28, ed. and trans. Bernard Sesboüé, with Georges-Matthieu de Durand and Louis Doutreleau [Paris: Les Éditions du Cerf, 1983].) It is on the basis of this intermediate structure of αἰών, this properly Trinitarian interval that one must interpret the "distension of the soul" (*distentionem animi*) Saint Augustine speaks of in his *Confessions*, XI; XXIII, 30; XXIV, 33 (cf. John Francis Callahan, "Basil of Caesarea: A New Source for St. Augustine's Theory of Time," *Harvard Studies in Classical Philology* 63 [1958]: 437–54). With respect to the terms αἰών and αἰώνιος in the Church Fathers, the reader will consult the *Theologisches Wörterbuch zum neuen Testament*. vol. 1, ed. Gerhard Kittel and Gerhard Friedrich (Stuttgart: Kohlhammer, 1957), 197–209 (art. by H.

in Homer.[35] However, what is important in this duration has less to do with its length, which for its part is relative, than the degree of its power; it is a "vital force," an internal principle of vitality.[36] While this force is limited in its duration—from birth

Sasse), as well as the work of A. P. Orbàn, *Les dénominations du monde chez les premiers auteurs chrétiens* (Nijmegen: Dekker & van de Vegt, 1970), chapters 3 and 4. Finally, for various uses of the term, such as αἰών οὗτος and αἰών μέλλων in the New Testament, one will consult the work of Oscar Cullmann, *Christ et le temps: Temps et histoire dans le christianisme primitif* (Neuchâtel: Delachaux & Niestlé, 1946), 31–35.

35. See, among others, the *Iliad*, V, 685, XVI, 453, and the *Odyssey*, V, 160; IX, 523 (cf. Benveniste, "Expressions indo-européennes de l'éternité," 107–8, and Hermann Fränkel, "Die Zeitauffassung in der Archaischen Griechischen Literatur," in *Wege und Formen frühgriechischen Denkens: Literarische und Philosophiegeschichtliche Studien* [München: C. H. Beck, 1960], 18).

36. As Benveniste writes, "Since αἰών is the internal principle that keeps the human alive, it is αἰών's persistence that will determine the duration of life, so long as a human's αἰών remains intact, so long will he live" ("Expressions indo-européennes de l'éternité," 109.) In Pindar's heroic songs, the αἰών, as the time of life, will at times be related to μόρισμος (fate) (*Olympian*, II, 9–11; *Isthmian*, VII, 40–42), at times to πότμος (destiny) (*Olympian*, IX, 59–61), and at times to the illustrated forms of survival:

> Having, by happy fortune, culled the fruit (τελευτᾶν) of the rite that releaseth from toil. And, while the body of all men is subject to over-mastering death, an *image of life* remaineth alive (ζωὸν δ᾽ ἔτι λείπεται αἰῶνος εἴδωλον), for it alone cometh from the gods. (Pindar, "The Survival of the Soul," in *The Odes of Pindar, Including the Principal Fragments*, trans. Sir John Sandys [London, William Heinemann, 1915], 589)

Consequently, without coming down to the eternal, immutable, and impassible life of the immortal gods, *aiōn* can mean the hero's *vital force* just as well as the *duration of his life*. But once the two meanings are separated, *aiōn* will lose its notion of power and will be reduced to the linear flux of an infinite time. The model of this infinity will no longer be *force*, but *number*, and *aiōn*, the son of time (Αἰών τε Χρόνου παῖς, according to the verse of Euripides just cited), will become the father of time (τὸν αἰῶνα αὐτόν ὅς ἐστιν τοῦ χρόνου πατήρ). Proclus, *In Platonis Rem publicam commentarii*, II, ed. Wilhelm Kroll (Amsterdam: Verlag Adolf M. Hackkert, 1901), 17. As Gilles Deleuze writes,

> whereas Chronos was limited and infinite, Aion is unlimited, the way that future and past are unlimited, and finite like the instant. Whereas Chronos was inseparable from circularity and its accidents—such as blockages or precipitations, explosions, disconnections and indurations—Aion stretches out in a straight line, limitless in either direction. Always already passed and eternally yet to come, Aion is the eternal truth of time: *pure*

to death—it seems unlimited in its power. It is without limit, for it is indefinitely reiterable and transmissible, from generation to generation, from past to present and present to future. It is a sort of eternal return of the "familial" generations, which will not have failed to define the continuous reversibility of the cosmic cycles on the physical plane.[37] But what about the term αἰών in the text of the *Timaeus*? Can we keep the idea of a lively force to define the nature of the model?

empty form of time. (*The Logic of Sense*, trans. Mark Lester with Charles Stivale [New York: Columbia University Press, 1990], 165; cf. 61 and 176)

While from Plato to Plotinus, all the way to Proclus, the clearest tendency will be to idealize the concept of *aiōn*, to separate it from any attachment to the sensible world, to isolate it from the world created by the demiurge and thus to attribute it a space outside any time, any change, and any movement, a sphere preserved and protected by the ideal laws of the model and by each of the categories of ideality (vision, intuition, identity, concept, sense, number, etc.), the Homeric occurrence of *aiōn* as life, or duration of life, however, will be found in Plato's text. "Polus: Many among men are the crafts experientially devised by experience, Chaerephon. Yes, it is experience that causes our times to march along the way of craft (ἐμπειρία μὲν γὰρ ποιει τὸν αἰωνα ἡμων πορεύσθαι κατὰ τέχνην)" (*Gorgias*, 448c; PCW, 794). Let us cite another passage from Aristotle's *On the Heavens*:

Hence whatever is there [the heaven], is of such a nature as not to occupy any place, nor does time age it; nor is there any change in any of the things which lie beyond the outermost motion; they continue through their entire duration (τὸν ἅπαντα αἰῶνα) unalterable and unmodified, living the best and most self-sufficient of lives. As a matter of fact, this word "duration" possessed a divine significance for the ancients; for the fulfillment which includes the period of life of any creature (τὸν τῆς ἑκάστου ζωῆς χρόνον), outside of which no natural development can fall, has been called its duration (αἰὼν ἑκάστου). On the same principle the fulfillment of the whole heaven, the fulfillment which includes all time and infinity, is duration (αἰών)—a name based upon the fact that it *is always* (ἀπὸ τοῦ ἀεὶ εἶναι)—being immortal and divine. From it derive the being and life (τὸ εἶναί τε καὶ ζῆν) which other things, some more or less articulately but others feebly, enjoy. (I, 9, 279a 23–25; ACW, 463)

37. Benveniste, "Expressions indo-européennes de l'éternité," 111–12. Plato, in the *Timaeus*, will for his part have directly linked the concept of *aiōn* to the regular and continuous cycles of the Perfect Year. It is thus not surprising that through Stoic speculations on the forms of the zodiac, the personalized figure of *Aiōn* would have been related by the Romans to the engineer of the Year, *Annus* or *Eniautos*, a sort of assessor of Dionysos *Cosmocrator* that protects and stimulates the seasonal cycles; it is the birth of the *aeternitas* legend. Incidentally, one

Or, more precisely, what should we retain from this idea to understand the living model both in its *ideal vitality* and its *specific temporality*? The lively force of the livingness of living things could be deemed unlimited (immutable, immortal, etc.) in this sense—and this is the only decisive criterion Plato provides on the subject of αἰών—that it must (always) remain within unity (μένει ἐν ἑνὶ)[38] (37b). Before being opposed to the time of succession, generation, and gradual degradation, the specific force of αἰών will thus be defined in accordance with unity. But Plato does not say that the living thing *is* a unity, but that it *remains* in unity. Beyond or before any noetic involvement or projection, the world of the Ideas *remains* one and the same world. In this sense, the living model would manifest itself *everywhere*—that is to say for each case of

will find in the Flavians certain inscriptions where eternity is personified as a woman holding symbols evoking *Sol* and *Luna*. See Louis Fourcher, "Annus and Aiôn," in *Aiôn: Le temps chez les Romains*, ed. R. Chevallier (Paris: Picard, 1976), 147–203.

38. This expression does not seem to have been used by any writer prior to Plato, or in any other work of Plato's (cf. Brague, *Du temps chez Platon et Aristote*, 30 and 58). One can nonetheless refer this to the sixth Nemean ode, where Pindar speaks of *ouranos* in these terms:

> One is the race of men, one is the race of gods, and from one mother do we both derive our breath; yet a power that is wholly sundered parteth us, in that one is naught, while for the other the brazen heaven *endureth as an abode unshaken for evermore* (ὁ δὲ χάλκεος ἀσφαλὲς αἰὲν ἔδος μένει οὐρανός). (Pindar, *The Odes of Pindar*, 369, emphasis added)

Aristotle for his part will use it to describe the state of the soul when it experiences no change:

> If, then, the non-realization of the existence of time happens to us when we do not distinguish any change (ὅταν μὴ ὁρίζωμεν μηδεμίαν μεταβολήν), but the mind seems to stay in one indivisible state (ἐν ἑνὶ καὶ ἀδιαιρέτῳ φαίνηται ἡ ψυχὴ μένειν), and when we perceive and distinguish we say time has elapsed, evidently time is not independent of movement and change. (*Physics*, IV, 11, 218b; ACW, 371)

The idea behind this expression can nonetheless be referred back to a certain passage on the concept of identity in the *Phaedo*: "the things that always remain the same and in the same state (ἀεὶ κατὰ ταὐτὰ καὶ ὡσαύτως ἔχει)" (78c; PCW, 69). See also 79a, 79d, 80b; *Republic*, 479a, 479e; *Sophist*, 249b; *Philebus*, 59c, 61e (cf. Joan Kung, "Why the Receptacle Is Not a Mirror," *Archiv für Geschichte der Philosophie* 70, no. 2 [1988]: 170–71).

participation by direct projection—and at every *moment*—that is to say for the entire projective and noetic duration of participation—in the form of a unit of reference and measurement.[39] Such a unit, consequently, would not be devoid of all time. Quite the contrary, it will constitute, "in" the duration of time, indeed "in" the duration of each time, whatever it may be—whether here or there, present, past, or future—a form that is *independent* from any object defined by time. It is the temporal dimension of a pure noetic content, a pure noema, as Husserl would say, a perfect intelligible that, while being directly and intrinsically involved by way of spontaneous participation in each of the demiurge's noetic aims, essentially remains devoid of objective localization and specific determination. The temporal form of the intelligible content of the model is thus at every moment *ubique et nusquam*. Having no place "in time"—either in the past or in the future—that is *properly* assigned to it, as is the case for any object of discursive thought and for any sensible affection, thus for any form of motion,[40] it will constitute, with respect to the noetic acts, whatever their quality may be, the indefinitely repeated form of a unity. This attribute thus does not represent the *contrary* of temporality, but a specific *mode* of temporality, and this is why we have chosen to translate αἰών by *omnitemporality*.

The living force of the model draws the form of its unity, its stable and autonomous form, from a structure that bestows an

---

39. While the context is different, one will find this idea of the numerical measure of time in Aristotle's *Physics*, book IV, 11, 219b et seq. (cf. Gloy, *Studien zur Platonischen Naturphilosophie im Timaios*, 63–64).

40. "Such notions we unthinkingly but incorrectly apply to omnitemporal being [*la substance omni-temporelle*] (ἐπὶ τὴν ἀίδιον οὐσίαν). For we say that it *was* and *is* and *will be*, but according to the true account only *is* is appropriately said of it. *Was* and *will be* are properly said about the becoming that passes in time (περὶ τὴν ἐν χρόνῳ γένεσιν ἰοῦσαν), for these two are motions" (*Timaeus*, 37e–38a; PCW, 1241, translation modified).

One could also cite the following passage: "And what is more, we also say things like these: that what has come to be *is* what has come to be, that what is coming to be *is* what is coming to be, and also that what will come to be *is* what will come to be, and that what is not *is* what is not. None of these expressions of ours is accurate" (38a-b; PCW, 1241). One will find the same sorts of difficulties on the subject of the τὸ μὴ ὄν ἔστι μὲ ὄν in the *Sophist*, 254d (cf. Harold Cherniss,

infinite power upon it, the power to be each time and every time "everywhere and nowhere." This power is a specifically numerical capacity: not only arithmetical in the strict sense of a discipline, but numerical in the strong sense of an ideality. When Plato speaks of the *nature* of the living thing (ἡ τοῦ ζῴου φύσις) (37*d*), he describes it as a αἰώνιον being, just like number, as it happens (37*d*), according to which the circular translation of the heavens unfolds. But, let us repeat, to describe the omnitemporal force of the living thing on the basis of a specifically numerical nature does not mean that every Idea can be defined as an arithmetical number. This means more precisely that only such a number can *make* the omnitemporal nature of the numerical ideality of the Ideas *intelligible*. This nature represents a principle of enumeration, a regulating term through the simultaneous iteration of stable units, a referential point of mensuration and recognition: in short, an absolute unit of measurement. But the αἰώνιος number, according to which the revolution of the heavens are measured, determined, and contemplated constitutes the arithmetical number—proper to each planetary revolution (the month for the Moon, the year for the Sun, and so forth up to the Perfect Year)—just as much as the pure unit of measurement of ideal number—in which the general revolution of the heavens participates, made visible through the enumeration of their circular motion. While the distinction between these two types of numbers is not explicitly marked in the passage concerning us, it nonetheless attests to a specifically

---

"*Timaeus* 38A 8–B 5," *Journal of Hellenistic Philosophy* 77, no. 1 [1957]: 342–43). Non-being was to be on the one hand distinguished from absolute non-being, Parmenides's οὐκ ὄν, and on the other hand from the non-being that is relative to being, a form of alterity just like the non-great for the small or the non-beautiful for the ugly (*Sophist*, 258c). It is the μὴ ὄν τι Aristotle will speak of (*Metaphysics*, 1003b; cf. 1003a). The imprecision, or the inaccuracy to which Plato alludes in the *Timaeus* concerns precisely the conceptual ambiguity between the absolute nothingness of time and its relative nothingness. Everything that becomes, was, or will be "is not" in the strictly ontological sense of *ousia*; yet each of these forms is relative to *ousia*. For us, however, there would still be an absolute nothingness of time, a nothing no longer relative to being or essence, but relative to time, a nothingness proper to this time we will have called originary, and thus "anterior" to the reciprocal ontological opposition of being and (relative) nothingness. Consequently, we do not know if we should say that this time is or that it is not.

Platonic conception.[41] This difference between number as an ideal unit of measurement and number as determinate relation of equation will allow us to understand how the heavens can represent the world of the Ideas.

The fact that the heavens are a visible being is heavy with consequences. In fact, once the heavens represent the world of Ideas, they above all allow one to *make* the participation of the world in the ideal numbers *intelligible*. They provide the means by which to understand in what the perfect structure of the world ideally consists. Their representative function thus constitutes a very specific noetic phase; they are, in the demiurge's projection, the *isolated moment* when the intelligible world is constituted in the effective form of a representation.

Once the heavenly bodies, illuminated by the Sun, make the motion animating them visible, they thereby make the numerical order of this motion intelligible, and it is thus that the heavens become the mobile image of the Ideas. It is thus not a matter, in this case, of motion itself, but of the number according to which its cause—the planets—move from one point to another. But this number—to take up Aristotelian terminology in a different context—is not a *numbered* number, without which the time of the planetary revolutions would be purely arithmetical, but rather a *numbering* number.[42] To be even more specific, one could say that

---

41. Cf. *Timaeus*, 37*a*. For all questions concerning the Platonic theory of ideal numbers, the identification or the subordination of the Ideas to numbers—of which we incidentally have nothing written down, except Aristotle's direct testimony (*Metaphysics*, N, 3, 1090*b*–1091*a*; Z, 11, 1036*b*; *On the Soul*, I, 2, 40*b*, *Eudemian Ethics*, 18, 1218*a*) and that of the Ancient Academy (Theophrastus, Hermodorus, Pseusippus and Xenocrates)—lastly, the reader will consult Marie-Dominique Richard, *L'enseignement oral de Platon* (Paris: Cerf, 1986), especially chapter 3, B, 205–10; J. C. Dumoncel's article "La théorie platonicienne des Idées-Nombres," *Revue de Philosophie Ancienne* 10, no. 1 (1992): 6 et seq.; and that of F. Fronterotta, "Une énigme platonicienne: La question des doctrines non-écrites," *Revue de Philosophie Ancienne* 11, no. 2 (1993): 115–37 (cf. Böhme, *Zeit und Zahl*, 130 et seq.). On the a priori structures of Platonic idealism, its figures and ideal numbers, see also Joseph Moreau, "L'Idée platonicienne et le réceptacle," *Revue Philosophique de Louvain* 86, no. 70 (1988): 137–41.

42. Cf. *Physics*, IV, 11, 219*b*. As Brague writes, "Time is not the number of movement, as Aristotle will say soon after. It is the movement of the heavens as it is regulated upon number" (*Du temps chez Platon et Aristote*, 63) (cf. John Francis

the number of motion in question here constitutes the *enumerable* (thus, properly speaking, neither enumerated nor enumerating) form of its enumerability into successive phases and regular periods. And this structural enumerability between the animate motion of the heavens and the lively force of the model, this pure enumeration of the intelligible becoming of the Ideas, is precisely what Plato designates with the concept of time.

§4. Aside the fact that it is a number, or rather, as we will see, something that falls under a numerical articulation, time was thus defined as, on the one hand, a begotten (γέγονεν) being, produced at the very moment (ἅμα) that the heavens were organized, and, on the other hand, as an act of representation (μίμησις), a mimetic operation through which the heavens became the image of omnitemporality. The concept of time thus involves at once a *numerical* form, a *genetic* form, and a *mimetic* form.

When Plato defines time as a number, what number is it? It cannot be a matter of *arithmetic number*, otherwise time would *ipso facto* come down to the sum of the elements it determines; time would become identical to the year, month, day, then to the hours, minutes, seconds, etc. Nothing would allow us to distinguish these terms from one another, and the motion of the entire heavens could neither represent nor manifest its participation in the world of Ideas; the demiurge's undertaking would thus have failed in its principle. But none of these numerically determinate periods defines time *itself*, but only *a certain* time. Incidentally, the number of time cannot be conceived of as an *ideal number*. Its numerical function, in fact, does not consist of remaining in the unity of one and the same present state, as is the case with the Idea-numbers, but further involves—let us emphasize this now

Callahan, *Four Views of Time in Ancient Philosophy* [Cambridge: Harvard University Press, 1948], 23). Number would thereby constitute a mediating principle between the heavens and the ideal model of the gods, a principle that would allow the ἀίδιον revolution of the heavens to never cease "imitating the model through the numbered or numerable force by which it moves itself." Léon Robin, *Les rapports de l'être et de la connaissance d'après Platon* (Paris: Presses Universitaires de France, 1957), 81 n. 37 (cf. Gloy, *Studien zur Platonischen Naturphilosophie im Timaios*, 65).

before returning to it below—a past dimension: a no longer being (present), and a future dimension: a not yet being (present). The number of time, properly speaking, would be neither arithmetical nor ideal. It would represent a sort of intermediary articulation, a definite, albeit modifiable numerical relation between the arithmetical sum of the months in the year, the days in the months (indeed of the hours in the days, etc.) and the indefinitely reiterable unit of measurement of numerical ideality, to which the determinate sum of each period in principle refers itself. Time would thus represent the *enumerable structure* of celestial motion. But let us not understand by this that time *enumerates* motion. The matter is much more complex. For it is time, and time alone, that constitutes the structure on the basis of which each motion can be enumerated differently *every time* all the while remaining one and the same motion—or the motion of one and the same planet. Time would thereby articulate a logical, numerically determinate relation for each planetary phase between, on the one hand, the motion of the heavens, or more precisely of what is *enumerable* in this motion (the years, the months, etc.), and, on the other, the unit of measurement of the ideal number it represents (the Perfect Year). And it is precisely thus that the heavens will become the mobile image of omnitemporality.

However, this enumerable structure, this temporal capacity of enumeration, even if properly attributed to the kinetic revolutions of the heavens, is a structure that is *internal* to the demiurgic organization of the world. While each of these motions can be indefinitely counted, its enumeration and intellection must in no way presuppose the existence of an already constituted heavens. For if the revolution of the heavens can be indefinitely enumerated, it is only because it is enumerable *by birth*; and it is precisely because it was born enumerable (and thus already temporally determinate) that it can continually organize itself in the numerical image of the Ideas. Its genetic enumerability would thus bear a productive order of representation. From this enumerable power to this mimetic function, time would thus constitute a double simultaneity. On the one hand, as we have seen, at the same time as the demiurge organizes the heavens (διακοσμῶν ἅμα οὐρανὸν), he makes of it an image of omnitemporality (37*d*) and, on the other hand, time and the heavens are born at the same time (ἅμα γεννηθέντες) (38*b*). As Plato writes,

for before the heavens came to be (οὐκ ὄντας πρὶν οὐρανὸν γενέσθαι), there were no days or nights, no months or years. But now, at the same time as he [*sc.* the demiurge] framed the heavens, he devised their coming to be (τότε ἅμα ἐκείνῳ συνισταμένῳ τὴν γένεσιν αὐτῶν μηχανᾶται). These are all parts of time (ταῦτα δὲ πάντα μέρη χρόνου). (37*e*; PCW, 1241)

This dual simultaneity between, on the one hand, the organization of the heavens and their representation and, on the other, the genesis of the heavens and that of time, in short falls under a single temporal operation. This operation, too, is simultaneous. But, differently from the first, this simultaneity unfolds between its capacity of making the revolution(s) of the heavens enumerable and its capacity to represent their numerical form. But, if time was born *at the same time* as the heavens were organized, and if, moreover, it was *in being organized* that the heavens became the image of the Ideas, how are we to understand the *birth* of time? What being or beings could have been born when time was begotten? If one answers quite simply "the heavens," one would thus distinguish these terms as two separate moments that would be reunited after the fact through a common unit of time. The genetic simultaneity of the heavens and time cannot, however, be understood as the coexistence of two determinate events; if there were such a gathering, a world, a space, and a time would thus already be presupposed. However, it is a matter of an at the very least originary simultaneity, and any predisposition of existence, and *a fortiori* coexistence would be excluded from it by definition. Furthermore, to understand how the genetic structure of time absolutely *coincides* with the productive representation of the heavens, one must ask to what extent time, understood between its force of enumeration and its mimetic function, is itself the factor of this coincidence.

The question thus becomes more complex, and the passage concerning us will not allow us to resolve this difficulty. But for the sake of clarity, and to close this first chapter, let us pose the problem anew. Time, for Plato, is at once *genetic, numerical, and mimetic*. It is important to understand its birth not as the fruit of a creative act—which is not in the demiurge's power—but as the representational genesis of a numerical organization. Let us recall that the heavens were ordered in the image of the Ideas when the demiurge inserted an intelligent and harmoniously proportioned soul into the body of the sensible world. From this insertion was born a gap in the mind of the god, between his *vision* of the world and the *ideal content* (the model) of his noetic aim. It is at the illuminated point of this gap, at this precise and distinct moment, that the idea came to the demiurge to represent this world in the form of a celestial vault. To put it otherwise, it is in organizing the representation of the world in the form of the heavens that the heavens could be temporally enumerated as a—henceforth numerical—image of omnitemporality. The time of the heavens, of their circular motion, of their continuous revolutions, of their successive periods, would consequently constitute the numerically organized representation of the noetic gap between the demiurge's vision and his aim.

Time is genetic, let us recall, not in the sense that it is born from the demiurge's force but in that it itself generates the demiurgic representation of the world. For, according to Plato, everything that moves in the heavens "are forms of time that have come to be (γέγονεν εἴδη)—time that imitates omnitemporality (χρόνου ταῦτα αἰῶνα μιμουμένου) and circles according to number (καὶ κατ᾿ ἀριθμὸν κυκλουμένου)" (38*a*; PCW, 1241, translation modified). This sentence could be a good argument in favor of the theory according to which it is time itself that constitutes the image of eternity. But one must not understand the χρόνου ταῦτα αἰῶνα μιμουμένου on the basis of the γέγονεν εἴδη, that is to say, in making the imitation of time something begotten in the same way as everything that moves in the heavens. On the contrary, one ought interpret this part of the sentence in accordance with the κατ᾿ ἀριθμὸν κυκλουμένου. In this way, in unfolding numerically, time can represent the begotten species of the heavens in the image of the Ideas. In other words, the imitation of time ought not be understood as a form of analogy but as a *productive operation*.[43] It is time itself that grants the living god's noetico-ideal

---

43. Cf. Brague, *Du temps chez Platon et Aristote*, 60.

projections the possibility of visibly enumerating, and making rigorously intelligible (to themselves), the logical relations of which the genesis of the world is composed. Not only does time provide the demiurge the means by which to grasp and represent his world as the heavens; it also allows him to understand that the numerical order upon which it is assembled from its birth, and by which it spontaneously participates of the Idea-numbers, is *already* an order determined by time. The genesis of time thus constitutes the precise *moment*—the moment of the gap—when the demiurge, his gaze incessantly fixed upon his model, understands, grudgingly, that (the representation of) his world will have always already been *temporally* assembled. In this instant, in this moment of delight, he would perceive that the time (or different times) by which the world moves as the heavens *coincides* exactly with the time of the building of the world. If this hypothesis holds weight, it would lead us to believe that there are two times of different natures. For, if it is true (1) that in organizing the heavens—or in inserting the self-moving soul into the world—the demiurge made of them an image of the Ideas, (2) that this kinetic organization operates according to the number of time, and (3) that the genesis of the heavens coincides with that of time, then the mimetic production of the heavens will be numerically determined by an order of time, and the time of the representation of the heavens will coincide point for point with the time of the building of the world, the world will thus well and truly have always already been a being *in* time.

§5. The heavenly bodies, Plato writes, are the instruments of time (ὄργανα χρόνου) (42*d*) or of the times (ὄργανα χρόνων) (41*e*). On the one hand, as we have seen, each planet, or more precisely each planetary motion, is assembled according to a certain time: so many planets, so many regular revolutions, and so many *determinate times* or *different times*.[44] But, on the other hand, once each of these westerly revolutions, after having equalized and

---

44. See Callahan, *Four Views of Time in Ancient Philosophy*, 21 (cf. Böhme, *Zeit und Zahl*, 145 et seq.). In a more general manner, Anaximander had already developed the idea of a particular time for each phenomenal generation: so many apparitions, so many determinate times (DK, *12 A 11*; TEGP, *10*, 52–53).

regulated their respective speed according to the easterly circle, will have returned to its starting point, their cooperation will realize a perfect number and thus the *unique time* of a Perfect Year. Plato clarifies a little earlier that the cooperation of the heavenly bodies should complete time (ἔδει συναπεργάζεσθαι χρόνον) (34e)—not to produce time in its genesis, but to realize a time in its greatest numerical perfection. That being said, if the heavenly body bears such a function, what are we to understand with respect to its being an *instrument* of time?[45] Is the heavenly body a tool for time, a means of labor and transmission? Wouldn't it rather be the organ, indeed more abstractly, the *organum* precisely through which time *represents* the order of the world as an organized heavens? Each planet would thus, in this case, constitute the *instrumental representative* of a determinate order. It would represent, one by one, and each specifically so, the temporal order according to which each of the revolutions of the heavens is enumerated. Without, however, defining the *order* of enumeration *itself*, it would serve as a numerical representative of the *determining unit* of this order.

Each planet will thereby determine a certain *relation* between the mimetic formation of time and its enumerating power. From this relation will be born the effective and visible distinction between on the one hand a stable unit of measurement, identical to itself at all times—this is the unit of the continuous *present*—and, on the other hand, the variable units of different times, which are the dimensions of the *past*—once the motion of one planet toward another has already happened—and of the *future*—when this motion is still to come.

> These are all parts of time, and *was* and *will be* (τό τ᾿ ἦν τό τ᾿ ἔσται) are forms of time that have come to be (χρόνου γεγονότα εἴδη). Such notions we unthinkingly but incorrectly apply to omnitemporal being. For we say that it *was* and *is* and *will be*, but ac-

---

45. According to Brague, each planet will constitute a particular instrument of mimesis, which will have time as its subject, αἰών as its model, and the heavens as its result (*Du temps chez Platon et Aristote*, 62; cf. Taylor, *A Commentary on Plato's Timaeus*, 258). One can thus say that the planets produce time in the sense that they complete, in their reciprocal assemblage, the numerical circularity of one and only trajectory: the Perfect Year.

cording to the true account only *is* (τὸ ἔστιν) is appropriately said of it. *Was* and *will be* are properly said about the becoming that passes in time (περὶ τὴν ἐν χρόνῳ γένεσιν ἰοῦσαν), for these two are motions. But that which is always changeless and motionless (τὸ δὲ ἀεὶ κατὰ ταὐτὰ ἔχον ἀκινήτως) cannot become either older or younger in the course of time—it neither ever became so, nor is it now such that it has become so, nor will it ever be so in the future.[46] (37*e*–38*a*; PCW, 1241, translation modified)

There would thus no longer be any external opposition between time and αἰών, but only a distinction internal to the continuity of time between the immutable present of a purely noetic existence and two horizons of non-being that correlatively correspond (past and future). Each planetary motion, at every instant, will involve and articulate the respective unit of this correlation.

Up to now, we have only located the function of time in the demiurgic production of the world. We have of course already been able to determine at what moment of this production the order of time allowed the demiurge to represent the world to himself in the image of the Ideas. We have nonetheless not managed to describe

---

46. See also 37*a* and 38*a*–*b* (cf. note 40 above). One should relate this passage to the concept of participation between the One and time developed in the second hypothesis of the *Parmenides*. The analysis plays out in three phases: What happens to the One and the other things if the One *is* in time (151*e*–154*e*)? What happens if the One *becomes* in time (154*e*–155*e*)? And, finally, how to determine this *time itself* (155*e*–157*b*)?

> "So when does it change [the one]? For it does not change while it is at rest or in motion, or while it is in time."—"Yes, you're quite right."
>
> "Is there, then, this queer thing (ἄτοπον τοῦτο) in which it might be, just when it changes (ὅτε μεταβάλλει)?"—"What queer thing?"—"The instant (ἐξαίφνης). The instant seems to signify something such that changing occurs from it to each of two states (ὡς ἐξ ἐκείνου μεταβάλλον εἰς ἑκάτερον). For a thing doesn't change from rest while rest continues, or from motion while motion continues. Rather, this queer creature, the instant, lurks between motion and rest (μεταξὺ τῆς κινήσεώς τε καὶ στάσεως)—being in no time at all (ἐν χρόνῳ οὐδενὶ οὖσα)—and to it and from it (καὶ εἰς ταύτην δὴ καὶ ἐκ ταύτης) the moving thing changes to resting and the resting thing changes to moving." (156*c*–*e*; PCW, 388)

Cf. Werner Beierwaltes, "'Exaiphnès' oder: Die Paradoxie des Augenblicks," *Philosophisches Jahrbuch* 74, no. 2 (1967); and Luc Brisson, "L'instant, le temps et l'éternité dans le *Parménide* (158e–157b) de Platon," *Dialogue* 9, no. 3 (1970).

the intrinsic structure of this representation. While this mimetic act is prescribed by each of the demiurge's noetic projections, its deployment would nonetheless involve an autonomous and rigorously defined thematic field. This representation should, on the one hand, perfect the resemblance of the world to the Ideas, and thus attempt to fill the infinite gap between sensible nature and intelligible nature, but on the other hand, this representation itself should also constitute the irreducibility of this gap. The mimetic act of time would thus represent at once, or simultaneously, the double noetic moment of the demiurge's noetic projections: (a) the moment when, delighted by the excellence of his product and his own power, the idea came to him to perfect its resemblance to the ideal model, and (b) the moment when he understood that it was no longer within his power to conflate this product with this ideality, and thus to spare the world an infinite expenditure, a total dispersion, and an absolute death. The representation of time would thus serve as the noetic gap between these two simultaneous moments.

Furthermore, with the aim of more precisely situating and defining the temporal genesis of the (numerical) representation of the world, between its sensible realm and its intelligible sphere, it becomes necessary to posit, or to postulate, a third term, a sort of intermediary that would be both constitutive of the elementary composition of the sensible world and necessary to relate this world to the omnitemporal model of the Ideas. Plato will have called this intermediary space χώρα.

Khōra

The Genesis of the World as Representation

The Genetic Formation of the Elements

The Internal Articulation of the Receptacle

§1. To determine the temporal genesis of the representation of the world, to describe the exact moment, within this genesis, when the linear becoming of the world changed into a representation, would require us to describe the concept of the beginning within the field of representation. That being said, it will not suffice to pose the genetic question of the world anew starting from an always already presupposed beginning, we will above all have to pose the problem of the beginning in terms of genesis. Plato did not only ask himself: "At which moment did the demiurge begin producing the world?" This question would only concern the material production of the world, its composition, assemblage, proportion, etc. The most decisive question should bear upon the conditions that allowed this beginning to *really* begin (48*a* et seq.). These conditions will precisely concern the mimetic production of the world. We must thus situate *another* beginning within the beginning of the genesis of the world, a beginning of the mimetic type that can no longer be solely reduced to the causal laws of the mechanisms of production.

The birth of the world issued from a mixture between an intelligent order and a mechanism of necessity. And, while we have seen that intelligence prevailed over necessity, while it was able to persuade its mechanism to *orient* the world toward the best of worlds, it was nonetheless impossible in principle for this intelligence to apply the perfection of the model to this world. But this impossibility seems intrinsically linked to the genetic orientation of the beginning. It is because the world is always already *oriented*, from the first moments of its birth, and thus destined in its principle to becoming a linear order, it is because it is condemned to indefinitely follow a single trajectory that it is radically separated from its ideal model—or, which comes down to the same, that it will attain this model in the infinite. But what happened *in* this beginning, and *since* the first moments of its evolution, so that such a becoming can and must unfold as representation?

§2. As Plato writes,

I shall have to retrace my steps, then (ὧδε οὖω πάλιν ἀναχωρητέον), and, armed with a second starting point that also applies to these same things (προσήκουσαν ἑτέραν ἀρχὴν αὖθις αὖ), I must go back once again to the beginning and start my present inquiry from there, just as I did with my earlier one (πάλιν ἀρκτέον ἀπ᾿ ἀρχῆς).[1] (48a-b; PCW, 1250–51)

---

1. This new beginning could be interpreted either in purely methodological terms, as a sort of technical precision, an argumentative revision or an improvement, or in ontological terms, as the elaboration of a principle of reason (cf. Gloy, *Studien zur Platonischen Naturphilosophie im* Timaios, 75; see also Taylor, *A Commentary on Plato's* Timaeus, 306, and Cornford, *Plato's Cosmology*, 161). In any case, one presupposes the empirical or ideal existence of a starting, originary principle. However, as we will see, the *khōra* that produces this new beginning is neither sensible nor intelligible. *Khōra* is thus a question of a principle without epistemic origin; it is a principle of pure differentiation, which only constitutes the conditions of possibility of an opposition between the sensible world and the intelligible world. It is incidentally interesting to note that Heidegger related the differential principle of the *khōra* to the ontological difference between being and beings:

An interpretation decisive (*eine massgebende Deutung*) for Western thought is that given by Plato. He says that between beings and Being there prevails (*bestehe*) the χωρισμός; ἡ χώρα is the *locus*, the site, the place (*der Ort*). Plato means to say: beings and Being are in different places. Particular beings and Being are differently located (*sind verschieden geortet*). Thus when Plato gives thought to the different location of beings and Being, he is asking for the totally different place of Being (*nach dem ganz anderen Ort des Seins*), as against the place of beings. (*What Is Called Thinking?* trans. J. Glenn Gray [New York: Harper Perennial, 2004], 227)

To take up this same beginning anew is thus to make another beginning of it (ἑτέραν ἀρχὴν). But, it is not a question of posing a second, older or more originary beginning, but rather of redefining its principles. The new beginning will be more differentiated than the first (ἔστω μειζόνως τῆς πρόσθεν διῃρημένη) (48e). Let us not thus understand this as a matter of simply nuancing its starting point. In a more radical sense, one must shift from an initial schema composed of two species (δύο εἴδη), or of two specific differences, the world and its model, toward a principle of differentiation—a dynamic articulation, a sort of differential spacing named χώρα that both *separates* and *enters into relation* the sensible world and the intelligible world.

There would thus be a third genus (τρίτον γένος) (48e, 52e), an intermediary, hybrid genus (52b) that one cannot—properly speaking—either grasp by the senses or teach to the mind (51e). Nonetheless inscribed within the sensible, and all the while participating of the world of the Ideas,[2] this genus would be invisible (ἀνόρατον), without form (ἄμορφον) (51a), and indestructible (φθορὰν οὐ προσδεχόμενον) (52b). Let us not believe for all that that this *khōra* represents nothing more than a negative term. It is the *khōra*, on the contrary, and it alone, that determines the *opposition* of the terms it excludes. If it is neither, in the strict sense, sensible *nor* intelligible, it seems to have just as much difficulty being defined as *both* sensible *and* intelligible[3] (52b). It would resist just as much the principle of exclusion as the laws of participation, whence its aporia among the most extreme (ἀπορώτατα) (51b).

This intermediary genus will nonetheless allow us to define, and then to structure, a very precise moment in the demiurge's production, the moment where the living god *takes hold of* (παραλαβὼν) (30a) this still indefinite mass of primary elements

---

2. Cf. Scheffel, *Aspekte des platonischen Cosmologie*, 62.

3. Derrida writes:

One cannot even say of it that it is *neither* this *nor* that or that it is *both* this *and* that. It is not enough to recall that *khōra* names neither this nor that, or, that *khōra* says this and that. The difficulty declared by Timaeus is shown in a different way: at times the *khōra* appears to be neither this nor that, at times both this and that. ("Khōra," in *On the Name*, ed. Thomas Dutoit, trans. Ian McLeod [Stanford: Stanford University Press, 1995], 89)

to make an ordered whole of it. While this moment of grasping represents the very first beginning of the building of the world, the very first contact between the demiurge's hand and this mass of energies, it will nonetheless remain dependent upon the mimetic conditions of this building. Of course, the heavens were not yet born when the demiurge took hold of the four elements; however, for reasons of principle, his action *would have already been directed* and his (noetic) production *already marked* by this medium without core and without extremity, by this infinite intermediary space where the elements of the world would become composed, assembled, and transformed in the image of the Ideas.

§3. Just as the Platonic Universe of linear becoming intended to distance itself from the ancient cosmologies and their reversible cycles, the basic form of such a Universe can no longer be conceived of in terms of an elementary structure. Plato's world is neither formed of the four elements (as with Empedocles), nor of a single element (water for Thales, air for Anaximander, earth for Xenophanes, fire for Heraclitus), or even Democritus's atoms.[4] The

---

4. One could, however, attempt to compare the Platonic *khōra* and Anaximander's *infinite principle* (τὸ ἄπειρον). This principle is an absolute principle, an origin without origin (τοῦ δὲ ἀπείρου οὐκ ἔστιν ἀρχή) (DK, *12 A 15*; TEGP, *16*, 54–55). Its infinity is just as *quantitative* (it is not determined either in height, length, or width) as *qualitative* (it is neither earth, water, air, nor fire) (DK, *12 A 9*; TEGP, *9*, 50–51). This infinite principle, moreover, contains a function one could further relate to the regulative operation of the *khōra*, defined in *Timaeus*, 52e–53b. It is an internal division to infinity (διάκρισις τοῦ ἀπείρου) (cf. Anaxagoras, DK, *59 A 41*; TEGP, *32*, 292–93), structured by an ἀίδιον movement (Anaximander, DK, *12 A 10*; TEGP, *19*, 56–57, see also DK *12 A 12*; not in TEGP), a division that indefinitely produces the genesis of every phenomenal appearance (DK, *12 A 10*; TEGP, *19*, 56-7) and at the same time proportionally regulates the reciprocity between each of these appearances. Just like Plato's *khōra*, Anaximander's infinite principle will constitute the pre-genetic structure of phenomena, a structure on the basis of which the genetic opposition between the appearance and disappearance of a phenomenon becomes possible. Incidentally, it has not been lost on readers to relate the Platonic theory of the ἄπειρον, developed in the *Philebus* (especially 23c–26e), to the *khōra* of the *Timaeus*. However, although this concept of infinity is without limit (πέρας)—it is an intermediary between extremes, which allows it to be neither hot nor cold, neither great nor small—it is nevertheless produced by an external cause (αἰτία) (23d), a cause capable of determining a distinction between the infinite and the finite. The principle of the *khōra*

world would thus issue from a source that no one had yet sought until then.[5] It is a structure that does not consist in determining types of elements, but rather in defining the *genesis of the elements* (γένεσιν αὐτῶν) (48*b*), a process of constitution through which each element will be able not only to be defined, at any moment, as *such* an element (as fire, air, water, or earth), but further become transformed under the aspect of *another* element. This process would thus be directly linked to the primary schema of the elementary corpuscles. It would constitute a reservoir of genetic potentiality at the nuclear center of each of these, a reserve whose power (δύναμις) will not be unevenly distributed, as one might be led to believe, but genetically oriented. This power, in fact, specifically has this—and as specifically genetic: it structures a sort of

---

for its part will be said to be infinite, not in the sense of a specific difference with respect to the finite, as in the *Philebus*, but in the sense that each new distinction, each new opposition will always presuppose a principle of differentiation without cause or origin—at least without any origin that could be determined before the opposition of the differentiated terms. For such a comparison, the reader will consult C. J. De Vogel's article "Théorie de l'ἄπειρον chez Platon et dans la tradition platonicienne," *Revue Philosophique* 149 (1959): 22–23 (cf. Victor Brochard, "Le devenir dans la philosophie de Platon," in *Études de philosophie ancienne et de philosophie moderne* [Paris: Vrin 1974], 108–9). Let us further note that Aristotle will one the one hand have identified his concept of matter (ὕλη) *as cause* (*Physics*, III, 7, 207*b*) with Anaximander's infinite (*Physics*, III, 8, 208*a*)—which for its part is not a cause—and on the other hand have alleged that Plato had himself conflated matter and *khōra* (*Physics*, IV, 209*b*, and *On Generation and Corruption*, II, 1, 329*a*; cf. *Physics*, I, 9, 192*a*, and *Metaphysics*, I, 7,988*a*)—which itself is also not a cause. See on this subject the work of Gloy, *Studien zur Platonischen Naturphilosophie im* Timaios, 82–89.

5. Mugler writes:

> In other words, in Plato's physics, the atom in the ancient sense of the word is not the ultimate reality that sensible appearances come down to. The atom itself, the ultimate fragment of corporeity, gives way to a more fundamental and more distant reality behind it, and "anterior" to it, the incorporeal, yet spatial substratum of the *peras*, by means of which Plato will constitute the elements and the mechanism of their transformations. (*La physique de Platon*, 213)

Cf., by the same author, "Le κένον de Platon et le πάντα ὁμοῦ d'Anaxagore," *Revue des Études Grecques* 80, no. 379 (1967): 217; R. Omez, "La notion platonicienne de la *chora*," *Revue des Sciences Philosophiques et Théologiques* 14 (1925): 438; and Joubaud, *Le corps humain*, 35–36. On the concept of immobilism as a principle, common among the mechanists, see *Laws*, X, 895*a*.

regulatory prescription, an assemblage that would be preliminary to any elementary composition and to each of its future transformations.

It does not directly determine the *linear becoming* of the elements—which, for its part, depends upon the purely physical bi-polar (centrifugal-centripetal) laws we spoke of above—but it forces the orientation of its genesis to *represent* itself as an infinite line. This power would thus in a sense constitute the *becoming-representation* of the elementary organization of the world.

That being said, how can one define such a power, and how to convince oneself that a genus so difficult to discern, so indistinct (χαλεπὸν καὶ ἀμυδρὸν), might contain a power that would be proper to it? It is not a matter of an elementary principle, or a basic substance, but of a pure *receptacle*. It is this receptacle, this power that *receives* in the manner of a nutritive source everything that is begotten (πάσης εἶναι γενέσεως ὑποδοχὴν αὐτὴν οἷον τιθήνην) (49*a*). Plato does not say that this power is both a receptacle *and* a wet nurse, as one might translate it, but that its capacity to receive the begotten beings is structured *in accordance with* a nutritive act.[6] Whence the inescapable example, indeed the model (and not the image) of the mother (μήτηρ)[7] and of the nourishing body (τροφός).[8] Ὑποδοχή comes from the verb δέχεσθαι, which means to receive, welcome, shelter, accept: its translation by "receptacle" is thus apt on a number of levels. It is the site where one receives, where one shelters, where one seeks refuge and asylum, such as the guardian of the laws in a sacred temple.[9] With respect to the

---

6. Cf. Brisson, *Le même et l'autre*, 210–13.

7. "This, of course, is the reason why we shouldn't call the mother or receptacle (μητέρα καὶ ὑποδοχὴν) of what has come to be, of what is visible or perceivable in every other way, either earth or air, fire or water, or any of their compounds or their constituents" (51*a*; PCW, 1254). With respect to knowing whether this figure of the mother can be defined as one of the attributes of the χώρα—which is supposed to have nothing proper to it—see again Derrida, "Khōra," 97.

8. Plato will still identify τιθήνη and τροφός in *Timaeus*, 88*d* (cf. Omez, "La notion platonicienne de la chora," 439). On the different images of the *khōra*, such as the golden object built by the goldsmith (50*a-b*), the wax or clay of the modeler (50*e*), and the perfumer's action (50*e*), the reader will consult Aloys de Marignac, *Imagination et dialectique: Essai sur l'expression du spirituel par l'image dans les Dialogues de Platon* (Paris: Les Belles Lettres, 1951), 35.

9. In the *Laws*, the term *receptacle* can either have the sense of a friendly welcoming, a welcome reserved to foreigners (ξένων ὑποδοχῆς) (XII, 949*e*),

substantive τιθήνη, before expressing what nourishes or gives to be eaten, designates what gives itself to be suckled,[10] what brings to the mouth of the begotten being what it needs to grow and develop. The gesture of τιθήνησις would not, first and foremost, qualify the fact of nourishing, but the direct transfusion of nourishment. In the strict sense, it is not to nourish a child but to give one's breast to the lips of a child. The care that the receptacle brings to the begotten being is thus a specific form of care. The receptacle reveals itself as protective, it tends to this being and nourishes it, not insofar as it is itself nourishment (τροφή) but insofar as it *brings* this nourishment precisely where this being needs it. Given this, what exactly could such a power of reception mean in such a context?

The receptacle of the *khōra* must be assembled in such a way that each of the elements it welcomes and shelters be protected *within* its genesis. This does not mean, first of all, that it is necessary to nourish and regenerate the elements already formed. *Khōra* is not a regenerator of energy, but the *site* of the transmission of energy. It is *khōra*, in fact, that carries, shifts, and provides energy to ensure the genesis of the elements. Its primordial receptive function thus does not consist in maintaining the equilibrium of the elements, but in forming the unfolding of their own genesis, which is quite different. The maintaining of equilibrium depends upon the cycles of transformation (their continuous reproduction and the conservation of energy), while the formation of genesis depends upon the linear becoming of these cycles (their slow but gradual dispersion). One must thus distinguish two things:

---

the sheltering of an exiled person (φυγάδος δὲ ὑποδοχῆς) (XII, 955*b*), or serve to designate the shelter for the guardians of the sacred temples (τοῖς φρουροῖς ὑποδοχὴν) (VIII, 848*e*). Cf. Olivier Reverdin, *La religion de la cité platonicienne* (Paris: E. de Boccard, 1945), 235.

10. Τιθήνεω, I nourish, I heal, comes from θάω, I suck, I suckle; θάομαι, I make suckle, I breast-feed (rad. θᾱ and indo-european root *dhe-*). Out of this would have issued both the substantive ἡ θήλη, the tip of the beast, the teat, the nipple, and the adjective θῆλυς, feminine, effeminate, etc. (cf. Chantraine, *Dictionnaire étymologique de la langue grecque*, 434, 2–435, 1). The root *dhe-* can be found in the latin *felāre* and in the French *fellation*. For this feminine principle in the context of the *Timaeus*, see Cornford, *Plato's Cosmology*, 357 n. 2, and Brisson, *Le même et l'autre*, 209 et seq.

(1) the *physical* laws that constitute every element as a body in becoming, and (2) the *genetic* laws determining the (linear) orientation of such a becoming. Furthermore, protecting the genesis of the elements would consist in structuring these elements according to a single orientation, which, once again, implies a simultaneous dual operation. It will be a matter on the one hand of ensuring the genetic unfolding of the elements—in other words, to see to it that the internal structure (the primary schema) of each element can continuously transform itself into the form of another element—all the while maintaining the genetic possibility of recovering its initial form later on. Short of this, the becoming of the world by way of continuous modification would have never been possible. But, on the other hand, it will be necessary to protect the becoming of the elements from its own dissolution, that is to say, to ensure that the linear orientation of becoming not be immediately reduced to systematic and total dispersion, failing which the order of the world, this time, will never be able to resemble the Ideas.

But how must one understand this dual (simultaneous) operation of the receptacle? How can one ensure that the genesis of the elements unfold the orientation of a linear becoming and at the same time protect this becoming from the laws (of orientation) of its own genesis? We have here a quite complex problem that we cannot stress enough. Here, one would be in the presence of a displacement that would be internal to the genesis of the elements, a spacing (χωρισμός), an inherent distancing to any linear organization. Indeed, once the receptacle protects the genesis of the elements it receives, it *displaces* their orientation. But it does not at all do so toward another site, nor even in view of another end, but in the form of a *representation*. In conformance with the strict sense of the τιθήνη, the receptacle of the *khōra* must provide the genesis of the elements with *what* they need *where and when* this need manifests itself—to put it otherwise, once their genesis commits them to a state of total dispersion. This critical point is not an accident of genesis but a constitutive structure that determines its own linear orientation, a structure through which the cycle of the elementary transformations is constituted (according to a systematic circuit) and dispersed (gradually exhausted) from the first moments of its genesis. Earlier, we situated this meeting point at the limit of the restorative force of the elements (between the centripetal force of the Earth and the centrifugal form of fire). And each time this force loses an irreducible minimum of energy through such a transformation, so each time becoming is oriented toward a death that is just as imminent as it is infinitely distanced, the receptacle of the *khōra* receives the genesis of the elements as an *imprint*, as a sort of typographic impression that structures each of the elements in the form of a determinate representation.

The *Khōra* and Its Representation

§1. *Khōra* will never be able to entirely exhaust the powers proper to it (ἐκ γὰρ τῆς ἑαυτῆς τὸ παράπαν οὐκ ἐξίσταται δυνάμεως) (50*b*). These powers order the form of a receptacle, and this receptacle has as its function the protection of the genesis of the elements, in ensuring the orientation of this genesis all the while protecting it from the irreversible becoming of this orientation. This is why the aporetic structure of the receptacle cannot be defined in terms of elementary forms, *substratum*, foundation, or even atoms, as a first cause. In fact, one cannot say of the receptacle that it determines that *on the basis of which* (ἐξ οὗ) the elements are constituted, as is the case for any principle. One, on the contrary, ought to define it as that *within which* (ἐν ᾧ) (50*d*) each of them becomes represented in the form of this or that element.[11] Properly speaking, the receptacle's protective function would be neither causal nor simply constitutive, but rather *representational*. It would protect the genesis of the bodies it receives in providing this genesis the representation its becoming needs to continually orient itself without immediately exhausting itself. Plato writes:

> Its nature is to be available for anything to make its impression upon (ἐκμαγεῖον γὰρ φύσει παντὶ κεῖται), and it is modified,

---

11. On the ἐν ᾧ as determination of the *khōra*, see 49*e*–50*a*, 50*d*, 52*a*, 52*b*. Cf. Brisson, *Le même et l'autre*, 215; Hans-Georg Gadamer, "Idea and Reality in Plato's *Timaeus*," in *Dialogue and Dialectic: Eight Hermeneutical Studies on Plato*, trans. P. Christopher Smith (New Haven: Yale University Press, 1980), 175; and especially Cherniss, "Timaeus 38*A* 8–*B* 5," 364–75.

Khōra

shaped and reshaped by the things that enter it (κινούμενόν τε καὶ διασχηματιζόμενον ὑπὸ τῶν εἰσιόντων). These are the things that make it appear different at different times (φαίνεται δὲ δι᾽ ἐκεῖνα ἄλλοτε ἀλλοῖον). The things that enter and leave it are imitations of those things that always are (τῶν ὄντων ἀεὶ μιμήματα), imprinted after their likeness (τυπωθέντα ἀπ᾽ αὐτῶν) in a marvelous way that is hard to describe. This is something we shall pursue at another time. (50c; PCW, 1253)

This passage reveals the mobile dimension of the receptacle, its intrinsic spacing, and, as we shall see below, its properly temporal articulation. But, for now, let us be content with precisely circumscribing the concept of representation.[12] The μιμήματα are defined here as so many elementary mimetic representatives, which must be situated at the intersection of three other notions. First of all, the *genetic motion* of the elements that enter and exit the receptacle, then the *omnitemporal beings* this motion represents, and finally the *impression* that such a representation leaves upon the receptacle. With respect to this term, it would be important to further distinguish on the one hand the τύπος (from τυπωθέντα), the *forma impressa*, the hollow mold—this guardian of memory spoken of in the *Theateatus*[13]—and, on the other, the ἐκτύπωμα (the

---

12. We will distinguish below the *khōra*'s genetic representation from the demiurge's noetic representation, his representation of the world as the starry heavens.

13. 191c; cf. note 1 in Auguste Diès's French translation of *Théétète* (Paris: Les Belles Lettres, 1963), 236. In the rigorous sense, developed in the *Phaedrus*, the memory in the typographical principle of the *khōra* would not be a simple reminiscence (ἀνάμνησις), a simple memory (μνήμη) (247d). The *Phaedrus* will have thematized the concept of memory in accordance with the myth of the soul, and reminiscence would thereby constitute a transposition from belief in metempsychosis into the theory of the Ideas (cf. Léon Robin, "Sur la doctine de la réminiscence," *Revue des Études Grecques* 32, no. 146 (1914): 451–61, reprinted in *La pensée hellénique: Des origines à Épicure* (Paris: Presses Universitaires de France, 1967). Jean-Pierre Vernant writes:

Platonic memory has lost its mythic aspect: *anamnesis* no longer brings back from beyond the memory of previous lives. But it maintains, in its relations with the category of time and the notion of the soul, an analogous function to that lauded in the myth. It does not seek to make of the past as such an object of knowledge. It does not aim at ordering temporal experience; it wishes to surpass it. It makes of itself the instrument of a struggle against human time, which is revealed as pure flux, like the heraclitean

Khōra

ἀποτύπωμα in the *Theateatus*), the *imago expressa*, or the form accentuated by the τύπος of the imprint. And if Plato seems to experience so much difficulty in describing this impression, it is because it is not in fact the elements themselves (in their sensible materiality) that are imprinted upon the receptacle, but rather their own representation. In entering and exiting the receptacle, the genesis of the elements will let its representation form its imprint within the receptacle, rather than form its imprint therein as a stamp on a soft surface. In other words, in such an operation, the μιμήματα, the elementary representatives, would themselves constitute the *forma impressa* of the receptacle, the relief of an imprint able to keep in memory the image, *the imago expressa*, of the noetic content of the Ideas.

§2. The receptacle's representation is a genetic structure. It is neither the act of representing (the demiurge's noetic representation) nor the represented content (the noematic unit of the ideal model), but a constitutive moment internal to the genesis of the

---

domain of the πάντα ῥέει. In *anamnesis*, memory opposes it through the conquest of a knowledge able to transform human existence in relating it back to cosmic order and divine immutability. At the moment when the preoccupation with individual human salvation is proclaimed, the human seeks the path therein towards its integration into the whole. What it expects from memory is not the consciousness of its past, but the means with which to escape time and return to divinity. ("Aspects mythiques de la mémoire et du temps" [1959], in *Mythe et pensée chez les Grecs: Études de psychologie historique* [Paris: Maspero, 1965], 105)

Contrarily to the *Phaedrus*, the theory developed in the *Phaedo* (72e), *Meno* (81d–85d), the *Theateatus* (191d and 197d), and the *Philebus* (34b) would be directly linked to the epistemic forms of learning and the techniques of recollection (cf. Michèle Simondon, *La mémoire et l'oubli dans la pensée grecque jusqu'à la fin du Ve siècle avant J.-C.* [Paris: Les Belles Lettres, 1982], 311–14; and Frances A. Yates, *Selected Works*, vol. 3, *The Art of Memory* [London: Routledge, 1999], 36–39). This opposition, proper to the constituting principle of memory, between on the one hand a *memory of being* (reminiscence as the rational constitution, or rationalization of any appearance) and, on the other, the *memory of the past* (memory as the temporal constitution of the becoming of every appearance) will find itself transposed in the *Timaeus* in the form of the genetic concept of representation. This concept will determine the mimetic inscription of an elementary formation in continuous mutation just as much as the mimetic inscription of an a priori genesis of constitution.

elements. This representation will allow both the deployment of the (specific) becoming of each element and the preservation, each and every time, of the memory of their own genesis. It is this representation, consequently, that maintains the receptacle's protective power. It is obviously just as difficult to understand the manner in which the force of the *khōra* can "inexhaustibly" provide a genetic representation of the elements as it is to grasp in what this representation can preserve the memory of this genesis. This is nonetheless what we must now attempt to explain.

According to our hypothesis, if the receptacle's representation can be defined as a genetic operation, this does not mean that it produces the genesis of the elements, but first and foremost that it genetically *relates* and *articulates* the linear orientation of the elements to and with the omnitemporal forms of the Ideas. Moreover, the properly mimetic function of representation bears an internal force of *displacement*, a force that allows it to intrinsically displace the linear orientation of this genesis toward the image of an ideal content. To ascertain and understand the principle of such a motion, let us recall that this genetic orientation would originally involve an irreducible loss of energy. We described above the physical causes of this consummation. According to our conclusions, however provisional, the force of cosmic restitution—the economic principle of conservation—was not up to the task of compensating for the losses of its own expenditure; However, one must now distinguish two points: on the one hand, the physical reasons that make it so that any energetic restitution itself presupposes a certain expenditure of energy, for which it will be necessary to appeal to another force of restitution, thus to another source of energy, *in infinitum*, whence the irreversible and gradual dissolution of the linear becoming of the sensible world; and on the other hand, the specifically temporal reasons for the irreversibility of the losses of energy, and this despite the fact that the numerico-temporal order of the cosmos has not yet been established. For if each energetic expenditure must be said to be irreversible, this does not *directly* depend upon the physical laws of restitution, which for their part only determine the properly cosmic consequences of dissolution (the continuous order of the elementary transformations).

If, somewhere, during the cycle of transformations, some energy is lost, if the genesis of the elementary bodies involves in its principle an irreducible minimum of expenditure, it is solely due to the linear becoming of its orientation, of its disappearance into a state of non-being or nothingness, and thus of its immediate and continuous fallout into an indeterminate form of time. Each time some energy is consumed, a minimum of loss in the lump sum of the cosmos seems irrecoverable. However, if there always remains a loss for which nothing can ever stand in, this loss will not for all that depend on the *quantum* of consumed energy. For it is not the consummation of energy that provokes the impossible restitution of its loss, but precisely the reverse, as if it were *necessarily impossible* to (temporally) recover these losses—to restitute them in all their singularity—in order that energy might be consumed, in order that a cycle of transformation might unfold, in order that a force of restitution might be constituted and that a world might be organized in the most perfect of autonomies.

And it is there, at this point of no return, that one must situate the temporal imperative of consummation: a sort of originary temporality, the ambiguity of which we will emphasize below. For it is not impossible, of course, to recover lost *energy*; any quantity of energy can in principle be restituted. However, it is impossible to recover the singular *losses* of this energy. Even if they express a certain *quantum* of expenditure, these losses—before any objective constitution of the world—will make of their energy a sort of absolute nothingness or "irreversible past." What is thus irreducibly lost in originary time, in this time of irreversible expenditure and pure consummation, is thus not an abstract *quantum* of energy but a concrete part of *this particular* energy, not directly, for example, a *quantity* of fire, but first and foremost a determinate part of *this* fire. And it is precisely because each elementary expenditure—in its singularity—presupposes a horizon of death, a past state that is forever lost and thus an *irreducible genetic loss* that, according to the laws of physics, an *external* force of restitution is required, whether through another element (the compression of fire toward air and air toward water), or through a second identical element that is produced separately (the ignitive radiance of the heavenly bodies toward the ignitive compression of the elements).[14] And it is ultimately because this external source of restitution must always and forever appeal to the energy of *another* source that it can never totally—that is to say at all times—replace the expenditures provoked by the labor and erosion of such an operation. One can thus say, as a result, that the energetic limits of restitution constitute the effect and not the cause of the energetic losses of the elements—whence the essentially salutary role and rememorizing function of the receptacle.

For an element to unfold according to a schema proper to it, so that an elementary corpuscle of fire, for example, might at times proportionally transform itself into an air corpuscle, at other times return to its initial corpuscular form, it is not sufficient to continually recharge the energy expended by the motion of its constitution. In other words, for the production of the elements to be possible, the cycles of transformation must not be reduced to conserving the consumed energy; it is still necessary that each of these cycles contains within itself the *memory* of their genesis. This does not mean, let us repeat, that they reproduce the lost energy, but rather that they represent—in the linear becoming of each element—the *specific form* according to which each can be determined as this or that element. Furthermore, protecting the genesis of the elements can no longer mean recharging the expenditures of energy (its gradual fall into a state of stagnation) by way of another energy, but rather to save its own irreducible genetic losses (its disappearance into the nothingness of an immediate past) by means of a representation of its genesis. This reasoning is simple and non-reversible. If it is true that the genetic representation of the elements will *have always been capable* of keeping the memory of their own genesis, originarily and forever lost, that is to say, if it will have always already been able to imprint their form in the figure of the receptacle, then its imprint will be able to freely assemble itself in the image of the ideas.

§3. According to what has just been put forth, the nourishing function of the receptacle would consist in protecting the genesis of the elementary bodies from its own genetic losses, and thus from its own becoming or its own (linear) orientation into

---

14. Cf. Mugler, *La physique de Platon*, 216–17.

nothingness. This protection, this continuous provision of genetic nourishment, if one can say so, would be a representation of the rememorizing type, a representation constituting both the receptive force of the *khōra* and its nourishing source. That being said, we still do not know how the internal displacement of this representation is articulated: the properly extensive structure of the *khōra* by means of which the sensible world can just as well relate to the intelligible world as become radically separate from it.

This extensive structure allows the receptacle's representation to *displace* the linear and continuous orientation of elementary genesis in the imprinted form of its genetic imprint. However, under what conditions is this mimetic displacement (of remembrance) possible? As Plato writes,

> we also must understand that if the imprints (ἐκτύπωμα) are to be varied (ποικίλου), with all the varieties there to see (πάσας ποικιλίας), this thing upon which (ἐν ᾧ) the imprints are to be formed could not be well prepared for that role (ἂ ν παρεσκευασμένον εὖ) if it were not itself devoid of any of those characters (πλὴν ἄμορφον) that it is to receive from elsewhere (ὅσας μέλλοι δέχεσθαί ποθεν). (50d-e; PCW, 1253)

Therefore, what allows the protective force of the *khōra* to imprint the representation of the element it receives, or, more precisely, what allows this imprinted representation to *depict* each of the elements received in the resemblance of an Idea, requires that this receptacle never take the form of one of the figures it represents; otherwise the resemblance to the represented content will never be perfect but always partial, and we would inevitably fall back into Presocratic conceptions. Plato thus clarifies below that "the thing that is to receive in itself all the elemental kinds [*genres*] must be totally devoid of any characteristics (πάντων ἐκτὸς εἰδῶν)"[15] (50e; PCW, 1253). The entire difficulty of the problem would consist in defining this distancing. How can the *khōra* distance itself from

---

15. "In the same way, then, if the thing that is to receive repeatedly throughout its whole self the likenesses of the intelligible objects, the things which always are [*les êtres omni-temporels*]—if it is to do so successfully, then it ought to be devoid of any inherent characteristics of its own (πάντων ἐκτὸς ... τῶν εἰδῶν)" (*Timaeus*, 51a; PCW, 1253–54).

the forms in the figure of which it represents the elements of which it is the receptacle? This gap in short would resist any intelligible discernment; it does not constitute a veritable structure, but a sort of predisposition to any type of structuration and thus, as we will see, to any noetic or demiurgic representation. We will devote the last few paragraphs of this first part to defining such a problem.

Representation and Configuration

The Informal Figures of the *Khōra*

§1. To understand the articulation of this gap, one must first reinterpret the up to now strict and rigorous opposition between, on the one hand, the specific form of the elements (determined by their primary schema), and, on the other hand, the receptacle of the elements (defined in accordance with their genetic memory). It is not, of course, a matter of suppressing or even weakening this opposition, but simply one of displacing its respective limits. For this opposition is not carried out *between* the elements and the receptacle, but *within* the receptacle: precisely where and when the figure of the receptacle withdraws from the elements it represents. The receptacle, let us recall, is entered into motion and cut apart into figures (κινούμενόν τε καὶ διασχηματιζόμενον) (50c) by each of the bodies it receives. "Before" this figural cutting apart—whose mobility, as we will see, determines the mimetic possibility of an imprint—there was not yet any distinction between the elements and their receptacle. In cutting itself apart through a definite configuration, in one and the same move the *khōra* will be able to (a) distance itself from the elementary forms sketched out through its own figures and (b) represent the rule (of equation) according to which each element can change its primary schema (transforming the geometric assemblage of its own polyhedron) just as well as recover its initial structure after the fact. While the *khōra* is without form, it is not for all that devoid of σχήματα, figures, postures, or manners of being.[16] These χωρισταί figures can be defined as so

---

16. Cf. Cornford, *Plato's Cosmology*, 185 n. 1. The main accepted senses of the σχῆμα are: the exterior form of a body (*Cratylus*, 423a; *Critias*, 110a), the geometric figure (*Meno*, 75b), the aspect taken by the result of a process (*Phaedo*, 72b),

many specific *modalities*. In fact, they only determine the state in which, at any moment of its genesis, the representation of the element they receive, welcome, and protect is found. They only single out, within the *khōra*'s reception, on the one hand the temporary and momentary *specification* of the represented elements, this or that *aspect* of theirs determined according to the genetic degree of their transformation, and, on the other hand, *that in which* each of these temporary aspects can be specifically determined as the formal sketch of such an element.

However, this opposition, internal to the receptacle, invites us to clearly distinguish each of the terms composing its power of representation. In fact, one must not only guard against confusing the τύποι and the ἐκτυπώματοι, but further distinguish the μορφαί, the μιμήματα, and the σχήματα, which seems to require more finesse. The two first terms, as we have seen, involve a correlative difference between the mark impressed in the hollowing out of an imprint and the ideal content in the resemblance of which the imprinted image is sketched out. The three other terms will be articulated within this imprint. The *mimemes* constitute what is traced in the marking of the imprint, the *morphemes* the definite forms (through the primary scheme of the regular polyhedrons) that such a tracing represents, and the *skhēmata* the aspect under which mimetic representations can at any point figure the specificity of these represented forms. This last term is thus very difficult to define. It forms a part of the mimetic operation, and does so even though it comes down to neither the noetic act of representation (the demiurge's aim) nor the represented noematic content (the ideality of the model), or even with its own mimetic representatives (the world as an organized whole). It is this configured aspect that constitutes the *relation of representation* between the *forma impressa* and the *imago expressa*. It articulates this internal relation of the elements to the receptacle by itself, it produces this relation by constituting the possibility both of a relation and a gap between the sensible world and the intelligible world.

---

and the form of a living species (*Phaedrus*, 249*b*). On this subject, the reader will consult Charles Mugler's article, "ΕΞΙΣ, ΕΞΕΣΙΣ et ΣΧΗΜΑ chez Platon," *Revue des Études Grecques* 70, no. 329 (1957): especially 74–75 and 87 et seq.

The genesis of the elements is a continuous transformation. Each of them is decomposed and recomposed in the form of another element. The gradual compression of the elements—the centripetal force of the Earth face-to-face with the centrifugal force of the ignitive radiance of the heavenly bodies—assembles a closed circuit of genetic modifications—so much so that none of the elements ever appears in the same way each time (τούτων οὐδέποτε τῶν αὐτῶν ἑκάστων φανταζομένων) (49*d*). Moreover, how can one say that some element is *this or that* element? While one must necessarily designate each element through a name proper to it, "what we invariably observe becoming different at different times (ἀεὶ ὃ καθορῶμεν ἄλλοτε ἄλλῃ γιγνόμενον) . . . to characterize that . . . not as 'this' (τοῦτο), but each time what 'what is such' (τοιοῦτον)"[17] (49*d*; PCW, 1252). This is a matter of not only a specific quality but also momentary, passing, and thus (each time) a temporally *localized* one. It is the aspect under which, here and now, in the orientation of linear becoming, the temporally constituted and specifically determinate form of an element presents itself, or more precisely figures itself. In other words, the receptacle's representation presents figures under whose (configured) aspects the specific form of an element *appears*. These aspects must thus never be conflated with the elementary forms they each time specifically and momentarily configure. Otherwise, the representation of these aspects cannot present the genetic singularity of the appearance of the elements in their diverse configurations— whence the necessary and implicit distancing of the receptacle with respect to the elementary forms it represents.

Each time the genesis of an element appears, each time one of the receptacle's forms protects and shelters it from its own becoming, and thus from its temporal orientation, the momentary specificity of the element becomes *represented*. However, it is not the form of the element (determined by its primary schema) that appears differently every time—which would of course reduce

---

17. On this subject, the reader will consult Brisson, *Le même et l'autre*, 180 et seq. See also J. Moreau, *L'âme du monde de Platon aux Stoïciens* (Paris: Les Belles Lettres, 1939), reprinted (Hildesheim: Olms, 1981), 17; and Joubaud, *Le corps humain*, 30–31.

any schematism to the status of an arbitrary construction[18]—but rather the *aspect* under whose configuration this form is represented here and now. And only *that within which* the aspect of such an appearance is constituted can be defined as an authentic determining structure. But, Plato writes,

18. What preexists any elementary constitution and any schematic regulation can be defined as a potential configuration that determines the possible limits of a body in becoming and the possible connections between these limits. It is a matter of a whirling, purely differential force that would create the partitioning, opposition, and at the same time the correlation between an irrational state of the Universe and the rationalized whole of an order of the world. The image of the *sieve* must now serve as our model.

Now, as the wetnurse of becoming (γενέσεως τιθήνην) turns watery and fiery and receives the character of earth and air, and as it acquires all the properties that come with these characters, it takes on a variety of visible aspects, but because it is filled with powers that are neither similar nor evenly balanced, no part of it is in balance. It sways irregularly in every direction as it is shaken by those things (ἀλλ ἀνωμάλως πάντῃ ταλαντουμένην σείεσθαι μὲν ὑπ ἐκείνων αὐτήν), and being set in motion it in turn shakes them (κινουμένην δ αὖ πάλιν ἐκεῖνα σείειν). And as they are moved, they drift continually, some in one direction and others in others, separating from one another (τὰ δὲ κινούμενα ἄλλα ἄλλοτε ἀεὶ φέρεσθαι διακρινόμενα). They are winnowed out, as it were, like grain that is sifted by winnowing sieves (ὑπὸ τῶν πλοκάμων) or other such implements. They are carried off and settle down, the dense and heavy ones in one direction, the rare and light ones to another place.

That is how at the time the four elements were being shaken by the receiver (ὑπὸ τῆς δεξαμενῆς), which was itself agitating like a shaking machine, separating the elements most unlike each other furthest apart and pushing those most like each other closest together into the same region. This, of course, explains how these different elements came to occupy different regions of space, even before the universe was set in order and constituted from them at its coming to be. Indeed, it is a fact that before this took place the four elements all lacked proportion and measure (Καὶ τὸ μὲν δὴ πρὸ τούτου πάντα ταῦτ ἔχειν ἀλόγως καὶ ἀμέτρως), and at the time the ordering of the universe was undertaken (ὅτε δ ἐπεχειρεῖτο κοσμεῖσθαι τὸ πᾶν), fire, water, earth and air initially possessed certain traces of what they are now (ἴχνη μὲν ἔχοντα αὐτῶν ἄττα). They were indeed in the condition one would expect thoroughly god-forsaken things to be in. So, finding them in this natural condition (οὕτω δὴ τότε πεφυκότα), the first thing the god then did was to give them their distinctive shapes, using forms and numbers (ταῦτα πρῶτον διεσχηματίσατο εἴδεσί τε καὶ ἀριθμοῖς). (*Timaeus*, 52d–53b; PCW, 1255–56 translation modified; cf. Mohr, *The Platonic Cosmology*, 120–24, and n. 29)

that *in* which they appear to keep coming into being and *from* which they subsequently pass out of being (ἐν ᾧ δὲ ἐγγιγνόμενα ἀεὶ ἕκαστα αὐτῶν φαντάζεται καὶ πάλιν ἐκεῖθεν ἀπόλλυται), *that's* the only thing to refer to by means of the expressions "that" and "this" (τῷ τε τοῦτο καὶ τῷ τόδε). (49*e*–50*a*; PCW, 1252)

Because the appearing of an element is itself genetic, thus always in becoming, its form can *only* ever be represented under the aspect of a momentarily assembled and temporally localized configuration: whence the receptacle's determining function. For it is precisely the receptacle that determines the possibility of *inscribing* the genetic structure of an element in each of these configurations. Without this possibility of genetic inscription, no aspect of any configuration could figure the form of an element, and thus no element could ever recover, at the end of every cycle of transformation and through the effect of a force of restitution, its own primary schema—and the becoming of the world would have never been possible.

§2. Not only is the receptacle's configuration indefinitely varied, as we have seen, but the uninterrupted mobility of these modifications will determine the internal structure of its remembrance. While this may seem logical, can one say for all that that the rememorizing function of representation depends upon such a configuration as an effect depends upon its cause? Properly speaking, this would not be a matter of a dependency of the causal type but of a constitutive operation of representation. In order to be able to represent the aspect configured by the sketching or the tracing through which the form of an element appears, it does not suffice to stabilize this aspect and to imprint its character upon a sensible surface. Above all, it is necessary to represent the "genetic rule," the rule of the potential equation of the prescriptive elementary transformations, according to which such an aspect *can*—in the variety of its sketching—figure the form of a determinate element. And this is precisely why each of these aspects will be *configured*. Each of them will indeed *contain* the genetic structure, or the genetic regulation of potential transformations, that will allow it to specifically sketch out, each time, the determinate form of an element. This structure will constitute not only the development of a primary schema but also the conditions that grant this schema the power both to continually *modify* its articulation and to indefinitely *return* to its initial form. It is thus not the receptacle's representation itself, its *forma impressa,* that preserves the genetic memory of the elements, but indeed its own configuration.

We can neither perceive the mimetic configuration of the *khōra* through the senses nor purely grasp it by the mind; we can only apprehend it through a sort of hybrid, illegitimate reasoning (λογισμῷ τινι νόθῳ) (52*b*). How, then, does one define the internal structure of this third genus, and how does one establish the mimetic displacement of such a (regulatory) structure of configuration? In a very dense passage, Plato relates the apprehension of the *khōra* to the formation of a dream:

> We look at it [*sc.* the third genus] as in a dream (πρὸς ὃ δὴ καὶ ὀνειροπολοῦμεν βλέποντες) when we say that everything that exists must of necessity be somewhere (ἀναγκαῖον εἶναί που τὸ ὃν ἅπαν), in some place (ἔν τινι τόπῳ) and occupying some space (κατέχον χώραν τινά), and that that which doesn't exist somewhere, whether on earth or in heaven, doesn't exist at all (οὐδὲν εἶναι). (52*b*; PCW, 1255)

Let us note first of all that Plato does not in the strict sense compare perceiving the *khōra* to a dreaming state. Nor does he say that, in this case, to perceive is to dream. But he claims, much more subtly, that *in bringing* one's attention *to bear* upon the *khōra*, we *form* a dream. The *khōra* thus becomes neither the object nor the oneiric content of the dream, but rather what allows each of these perceptive aims to assemble itself in the form of a dream. This oneiric form of perception would constitute the only manner of knowing the *khōra*. But how must one understand this?

According to an old Orphico-Pythagorean tradition, to which Plato implicitly refers, the dream would be a type of divination (μαντεία).[19] The oneiric apperception of the *khōra* would thus

---

19. The theory of divination, elaborated in *Phaedrus,* 244*a* et seq., describes a type of knowledge that is very close to the dialectical method. Both would in their own way determine a path toward reminiscence. What divination does in particular is that it makes the divine intervene directly, when "[one's] power of

involve two points directly linked to the *mimetic* process of re-membrance: on the one hand, knowledge through an image, of the reproductive or analogical type (71*b*), and on the other a specifically temporal formation of this image (72*a*). The oneiric formation of images is distinctive in that, in the *present* and *continuous* state of its imprint, it involves both the possibility of returning to the *past* of the imagined content (of *rememorizing* the traits proper to it) and the possibility of anticipating the forms of this content that are *to come* (*foreseeing* their future assemblages). After having attributed the power of divination exclusively to diseases and fits of possession, and not to the reasonable state of the intellect, Plato writes this:

> On the other hand, it takes a man who has his wits about him to recall and ponder (Ἀλλὰ συννοῆσαι μὲν ἔμφρονος τά τε ῥηθέντα ἀναμνησθέντα) the pronouncements produced by this state of divination or possession (ὑπὸ τῆς μαντικῆς τε καὶ ἐνθουσιαστικῆς φύσεως), whether in sleep or while awake (ὄναρ ἢ ὕπαρ). It takes such a man to thoroughly analyze any and all visions (φαντάσματα) that are seen, to determine (λογισμῷ διελέσθαι) how and for whom

understanding (τὴν τῆς φρονήσεως . . . δύναμιν) is bound in sleep or by sickness, or when some sort of possession works a change (παραλλάξας) in him" (*Timaeus*, 71*e*; PCW, 1272). Just as rationality can be disturbed through an effect of possession and compensated through an intervention of the divine in divination, so too can reason—which during its waking state can only act upon the appetitive part of its soul through its most irascible part—in the dream rationally operate on the concupiscence of its soul (cf. Brisson, *Le même et l'autre*, 201–7). As E. R. Dodds writes,

> Plato in the *Timaeus* offers a curious explanation of mantic dreams: they originate from the insight of the rational soul, but are perceived by the irrational soul as images reflected on the smooth surface of the liver; hence their obscure symbolic character, which makes interpretation necessary. ("Dream-Pattern and Culture-Pattern," in *The Greeks and the Irrational* [Berkeley: University of California Press, 1951], 120)

Without thereby being subject to the forms of the sensible, it is nonetheless *within* the sensible that the oneiric state of the dream will be able to rationally determine the order of the sensible. The epistemic modality of the dream, from the remembrance of a previous state to the anticipation of a future one, would constitute a knowledge that would be halfway between a sensible and an intelligible knowledge—whence the relevance of its cognitive function in the *khōra*'s mimetic unfolding.

they signify some future, past or present good or evil (μέλλοντος ἢ παρελθόντος ἢ παρόντος). (71e–72a; PCW, 1272–73)

Following this, one can say that perceiving the *khōra* involves an oneiric function, for only the interpretation of a dream, the anterio-posterior vision of its representation, allows the articulation of a logical and continuous relation between the already past or already represented phases of the imprinted image and the possible phases of its modifications to come, from the nearest to the most distant. These primary and quasi-oneiric forms of temporality would in a sense constitute the origin of the very dimensions of natural and cosmic time (the time of the planets). Consequently, this oneiric function of remembrance alone can represent the linear becoming of the genesis of the elements.

There is thus no longer any possible confusion. The *khōra* must not be defined as an oneiric content but as a sort of constellation of figures, a configuration that forces any apprehension to unfold in an oneiric form—in a form capable of bringing together the anterioposterior dimensions of its apprehended object into a single point in time. This configuration, let us recall, involves something like a genetic memory of the elements. It allows each representation of their genesis to relate the momentary and temporal aspects of its phase to its respective form. However, such a relation does not depend upon a structure of the analogical or associative type, but upon a potential regulation that would be proper to the linear becoming of the elements, a potentiality that allows each elementary orientation to both (a) maintain, beyond its transformations, the genetic structure of its own scheme—to protect or guard its memory—and (b) anticipate the future changes of these transformations; and this not to multiply purely formal possibilities, but in view of regularly—and thus circularly or indefinitely—recovering the perfect identity of its initial structure.

While Plato does not directly speak of the genetic "anterioposteriority" of elementary becoming, we will nonetheless relate this structure to the principle according to which any visible body must necessarily manifest itself *in a certain site* (ἔν τινι τόπῳ)[20]

---

20. This is Zeno's principle, reported by Aristotle (*Physics*, IV, 1, 208a), a principle according to which "everything that is, is in a place (πᾶν τὸ ὂν ἐν τόπῳ)" (Zeno, DK, *19 A 24*; TEGP, *24*, 262–63).

(52*b*). Thus any configured aspect of the *khōra* would represent a determinate site: not a fixed and static point along an infinite line, but a *force of spacing* within the circular unity of the line. In each time differently figuring the form of an element, each of these aspects would represent the site of a genetic articulation—more precisely, the site where the anterio-posterior relation of the linear becoming of all generation is "originarily" articulated. And, just as this site is not a mathematical point, this relation will not be a simple series of successive points. This relation does not on its own determine the linear relation between a before and an after, between an element's anterior state—the basic scheme of its regular polyhedron—and the posterior state of its transformation—the change in equation between its primary triangles and the formation of a new regular polyhedron. This relation, on the contrary, constitutes the circular form of its continuous orientation, the possibility of inscribing within each phase of its trajectory the (chemico-mathematical) necessity of a regular return to the initial state of the elementary structures, whence the *momentary* co-implication of linear and circular motion, and consequently whence the *possibility* of representing, before any intervention on the demiurge's part, the linear becoming of the elements in the image of an ideal model.

The receptacle of the *khōra* would thus in a way constitute the site where, each time specifically, the genetic inscription of such a relation would be represented. This site of inscription or remembrance would form a double gap: (1) the gap separating the configured aspect of an element from the becoming of its primary genesis (or the specification of its form), and (2) the gap that separates this very aspect from the final product of its transformation—understood as the regular and circular product. If this site could not in itself situate the singular relation of the distances of these two gaps, if it could not continuously inscribe the genetic unity of this relation into each of the representations of an element, and thus keep a memory of it, none of the elements would have been able to shelter themselves from the genetic losses of their elaboration and each of them would consequently have never been anything other than a pure apparition or even a vain illusion. For, Plato writes, since that for which an image has come to be is not at all intrinsic to the image (οὐδ᾽ αὐτὸ τοῦτο ἐφ᾽ ᾧ γέγονεν ἑαυτῆς ἐστιν), which is invariably borne along to picture something else (ἑτέρου δέ τινος ἀεὶ φέρεται φάντασμα), it stands to reason that the image should therefore come to be *in* something else, somehow clinging to being (οὐσίας), or else be nothing at all (ἢ μηδὲν τὸ παράπαν αὐτὴν εἶναι). (52c; PCW, 1255)

Thanks to this site of reception, this site within which any appearance is represented, the image of the element will have been protected from the risk of being nothing other than a vain illusion, an image always at the mercy of the linear becoming of the elements. But because of such a reception, the image of the element will at the same time have been threatened with no longer being able to represent its genesis in the resemblance of the Ideas.

The *Khōra* and Its Force of Spacing

§1. We have just attempted a rather risky interpretation of the *khōra*. This term would be neither the principle of a cause nor the act of a constitution, but would determine first and foremost the rememorizing force of a representation. We will thus devote the second and final part of this study to describing the cosmological and anthropological consequences of such a determination. These consequences will be sizable: they will force us to pose the problem of the demiurgic building of the world more subtly. For, let us recall, before Plato describes the *khōra*, the demiurge had to produce the world—all the while representing its perfect order (to himself) as the starry heavens—by means of the available elements, charged with a determinate energy. But once these preliminary elements, received, protected, and begotten by the *khōra*, appear in an indefinite variation of configured aspects, the demiurge would never be able to directly grasp them in their specific material givenness. The appearance of an element always being fleeting and varied, the demiurge will have to take hold of their form only through the marked and imprinted traits of a representation. The elements at the demiurge's disposal would thus always already be in a *state of representation*, and consequently the representation he will make of the world to himself will always constitute the (cosmic) representation of an (elementary or genetic) representation. A *risk* of illusion will necessarily follow from this mimetic anteriority upon which the demiurge's own representation of the world is based. This representation of a representation will not have as its content an illusory object, but an object that carries an illusion; and, as we will see, this content will determine the necessity of a principle and of a mortal race within the organized whole of the Universe.

§2. The receptacle of the *khōra* is defined as a mimetic force of spacing, as a gap of representation within which the sensible world both distances itself from and comes closer to its ideal model. But this gap is not the result of this entering into relation. Quite the contrary, it is this gap alone that, from the moment of the genesis of the elements, articulates the possibility of inscribing such a relation within the linear becoming of any transformation. In order that each aspect of an element can be represented in the image of an Idea, it is indeed necessary that the configuration of the *khōra*—under whose traits the multiple appearances of any element are sketched out—have inscribed within it the (purely regulatory) *possibility* both of containing the memory of the genetic losses of the element and anticipating or foreseeing the conditions of a regular return to the initial state of its genesis; this is what we were calling originary time. We saw, however, that these genetic losses could never be compensated through the purely physical forces of a return of energy. These losses being singular, that is to say individually and irreducibly bound to the linear becoming of each element, the physical force of restitution will necessarily be foreign to them, the recourse to this other force of energy will itself involve a new expenditure of energy, for which it will once again be necessary to have recourse to another force, and so on indefinitely. It is thus not thanks to the physical forces of restitution (alone), and the regular return of the primary structures alone, that each element will be able to be genetically assembled in the image of the Ideas. In order that this resemblance not only be *possible* but *effective*, one must on the contrary have recourse to the mimetic forms of restitution. It is indeed necessary that the representation of this return be inscribed—as a *potentially defi-nite trace*—into the linear transformation of the elements, and this before any demiurgic organization of the world. This is what we were above calling the representational becoming of genesis, the representation of an infinitely potential curve in the orientation of a line. As Plato writes,

indeed, it is a fact that before this took place the four elements all lacked proportion and measure (ἀλόγως καὶ ἀμέτρως), and at the time the ordering of the universe was undertaken, fire, water, earth and air initially possessed certain traces of what they are now (ἴχνη μὲν ἔχοντα αὑτῶν ἄττα). They were indeed in the condition one would expect thoroughly god-forsaken things to be in. So, finding them in this natural condition (οὕτω δὴ τότε πεφυκότα), the first thing the god then did was to give them their distinctive shapes, using forms and numbers (ταῦτα πρῶτον διεσχηματίσατο εἴδεσί τε καὶ ἀριθμοῖς).[21] (53*a-b*; PCW, 1256 translation modified)

These traces of genetic imprinting, these forms sketched out by the genesis of the elements, will constitute the *mimetic possibil-ity* of an organization of the world. Without the possibility of these traces, without the possibility of effectively inscribing the delimited (anterio-posterior) horizon of a specific form within each fleeting and dispersed appearance of each element, the de-miurge would never have been able to take hold of the elements, with their stable contours, separated from one another. In no case would he have had the means to proportionally mix the elements according to their own structure; before him, this indefinite mass of elements could only have presented itself to him in a state of continuous quaking (σείεσθαι) (52*e*), of the most unstable turbu-lence and whirling.

The protective receptacle of the *khōra* would represent the force of the spacing of the (genetic) potentialities of this trace. Hence-forth, the demiurgic representation of the world, the birth of the heavens and of natural time, can no longer be defined according to the simple terms of reproduction. This representation will not

---

21. Cf. Kung, "Why the Receptacle Is Not a Mirror," 172.

have elementary datum as its mimetic representative, but rather the genetic representation of an already configured aspect of this datum. And, while the receptacle of the *khōra* should be able to protect the representation of the elements from the vanity of illusion, can one now say that, for the demiurge's representation, such a type of guarantee and legitimation exists? What is the agency that would allow these representations, the organized world and the starry heavens, to not be reducible to the purely illusory forms of an image? This is what we will now attempt to problematize.

2

The Phenomenological Formation of Time

3

The Genesis of Time and the Mimetic Functions of the Soul

Genetic Time and Numerical Time

The Order of the World and the Two Concepts of Representation

§1.

For the moment, we need to keep in mind three types of things: that which comes to be (τὸ μὲν γιγνόμενον), that in which it comes to be (τὸ δ᾽ ἐν ᾧ γίγνεται), and that after which the thing coming to be is modeled, and which is the source of its coming to be (τὸ δ᾽ ὅθεν ἀφομοιούμενον φύεται τὸ γιγνόμενον). It is in fact appropriate to compare the receiving thing to a mother (μητρί), the source to a father (πατρί), and the nature between them to their offspring (τὴν δὲ μεταξὺ τούτων φύσιν ἐκγόνῳ). (50c-d; PCW, 1253)

The passage above will now allow us to clarify the relation between the different moments of the production of the world: the genesis of the elements, the cosmic order of this genesis and, the representation of this order as the starry heavens. If the nature of the elements can be said to be an *intermediary* between the receptacle and the model, this productive relation can no longer be understood according to the laws of a gradual and continuous building alone, from the first elementary components to the final refinings of the Universe. When the demiurge took hold of the elements, these corpuscles were *already* potentially assembled in the image of the model, or, more precisely, each of them had *already received*, in the represented aspect of a specific form, the *possibility* of being formed and determined in the resemblance of the Ideas. These elements, consequently, must not be defined as given primary atoms, at the demiurge's disposal, but as intermediary phenomena, representations, whose respective form would be (genetically) predisposed toward the organization of the world.

In this way, since the demiurge can *represent* the world he produces *to himself*, if the idea can come to him to represent the perfect order of the world as the starry heavens, and thus to fashion it in the celestial image of the Ideas, it is thanks to these mimetic predispositions and to the essentially phenomenal aspect of the elements upon which it rests. However, as we have seen, as complete as this world may be, and as great as the demiurge's power might have been, the perfect application of this image to its model is impossible. An irreducible and infinite gap, as small as it may be, will always persist. One might have therefore thought that this gap occurred directly between this world and its model, and that the cause of such a gap thus directly issued from the mimetic nature of the world. But everything leads us to believe that this nature depends upon this gap, and not the reverse. In the strict sense, it is not because the world is mimetic that it can never measure up to its own model, but it is precisely because it can never measure up to it that it is mimetic in its very essence. The logic is thus quite different, and the relation between the world and the Ideas must no longer be reduced to the *hierarchical* opposition between a copy and its model. Plato's world is of course a copy of the Ideas, but its representation is not the simple degraded state of these Ideas. When the demiurge represents the world to himself as the starry heavens, this representation does not have as its content an image that would derive from the model, but precisely the irreducible *gap* between the sensible world and this ideal model. It is thus from this gap that the mimetic representation of the world will come about. But where does this gap issue from? It cannot be located at the level of the Ideas, since the copy-model opposition depends upon such a gap. There thus remains the lower threshold of the world, this phenomenal infrastructure upon which the mimetic ordering of the world rests and is founded.

We will thus attempt to situate the origin of this gap between the *genetic representation* of the elements (their structural phenomenality) and the *demiurgic representation* of the world (its noetic form), between, on the one hand, the regulatory potentiality of the linear becoming of the elements and the regular circularity of their transformation and, on the other hand, the planetary ordering of an armillary sphere. Each of these representations will represent its object in the image of the Ideas: the first by genetically inscribing the possibility of (indefinitely, but in a regular manner) recovering its primary form within each of the (phenomenal) aspects of the transformation of an element, the second by harmoniously animating and visibly structuring the order of the concentric layers of the sphere in a double circular motion, that of the same and that of the other. But the question now arises of how these two mimetic acts might relate to one another, and of what thus follows for the demiurgic representation of the world, for its soul and for the heavens, if this act is already in itself the (noetic) representation of a (phenomenal) representation.

§2. Let us recall that the representation of the elements refers to and is related to the phenomenal genesis of the reciprocal and continuous transformations between these elements. Furthermore, what we could call the *objective relation* of this representation—the relation that would allow any elementary appearance to—let us say objectively—*inscribe* itself into a determinate site, and thus to be articulated in a particular way, during the course of each of the genetic phases of its transformation, between preserving its primary form and anticipating a regular return to this form—the relation that would thus allow one to make of any *representation* the representation of *this particular* element, will be sheltered from the vain illusions through the protective power of the receptacle. In ensuring the "objectivity" of elementary representations, in ensuring that each of its sketches always and iterably constitutes the configured aspect of its own form, the *khōra* will become the potential guarantor of a resemblance between these elements and the Ideas. However, the same does not hold for the demiurgic representation of the world. The relation this act would undertake with respect to its represented object (its noematic content, that is to say, the ideal ordering of the world) is not effectively inscribed into the genetic structure of this object. While the genesis of the world is organized by way of representation, while the representation of the world as the heavens in some way coincides with its production as an ordered whole, this representation is not properly speaking *genetic*—whence the irreducible distance between the represented object and its objective relation. One must insist on such a distinction. The representation of the world in fact does not concern the proportional laws of its genesis. The demiurge can only represent its perfect organization to himself by inserting an intelligent soul into its already constituted sensible body. From here would issue the irreducible dependence of the world upon the wills and powers of the demiurge, and from here consequently would ensue the inevitable risk of a purely noetic illusion, an illusion of the transcendental type.

The representation of the elements is *genetic* and its temporality properly *phenomenal*; it is potentially inscribed into their own structure and effectively guaranteed by the protective force of the *khōra*. The representation of the world, by contrast, is *noetic*, its temporality determined by a properly *cosmological* order; it directly depends upon the demiurge's intentions and is limited to the capacities of his productive intelligence. The world will remain in the image of an Idea so long as the god wills it, so long that he produces its harmonious organization, and consequently for as much time as he, the all-powerful, will be able to *represent* this harmony in the image of the Ideas. The demiurge's transcendental illusion would thus carry with it a double risk. While the genetic representation of the elements allows each of them to become assembled in the image of the Ideas, this structure will nonetheless remain purely potential; it will only define these elements as *ideally representable* beings, and not *effectively represented*. Nothing in them should *oblige* the demiurge to take hold of their bodies to effectively order them in the image of the Ideas. Without the demiurge's productive intervention, this power would of course remain as hollow as it would be formal, and nothing more could prevent the linear becoming of the elements to dissolve, to disappear at the limit of a slow but certain death. Of course, once the demiurge had the intention of producing the world, he necessarily had to resort to the mimetic power of the elements. This noetic intention, however, does not depend upon this power. On the one hand, the world could very well have not existed and never have been represented in the image of the model—due to the strict mimetic potentiality of the elements upon which it is founded—and, on the other hand, this same world could one day no longer be represented in this image and thus no longer exist as an organized world; it could thus gradually dissolve up to its total annihilation—this time only because of the demiurge's volitional power.[1] While the demiurge is capable of producing the world, and thus spare it the potential risk of never having existed, it remains to be seen *for how long* this living god will be able to maintain the intentional and noetic rigor of his own will.

The Demiurge's Last Will

§1. As we have seen, the demiurge's goodwill constitutes a stronger and more powerful bond (δεσμοῦ καὶ κυριωτέρου) than those by which the begotten creatures were bound on the day of their birth (41*b*). Nonetheless, the demiurge says, "you, as creatures that have come to be, are neither completely immortal (ἀθάνατοι μὲν οὐκ ἐστὲ) nor exempt from being undone (οὐδ᾽ ἄλυτοι τὸ πάμπαν)" (41*b*; PCW, 1244). Of course, the demiurge's *goodness* would forbid him from willfully breaking such harmonious bonds (41*b*). But is this goodness sufficiently decisive to shelter his voluntary actions and his most deliberate intentions from the limitations of his own power? Is this power thus capable of guarding his representation from all illusory phenomena? In order that these actions might ensure an absolute indissolubility to the world—or an indissolubility in principle—it will have been necessary that this power might, at any point in time, ensure its perfect adequacy

---

1. There would thus be a *triple potentiality* of the world: (1) the *genetic* potentiality of the elements (the world could have never existed or never been represented in the image of the Ideas), (2) the demiurge's *noetic* potentiality (the world could one day no longer exist or no longer be represented in the image of the Ideas), and (3) the purely *mimetic* potentiality of a representation of a representation; this is the power to noetically represent the genetic representation of the elements in the cosmic form of the starry heavens. This power will consequently determine the noetic limits of the demiurge's productive capacities.

97

to the model of the Ideas, which the demiurge is incapable of, by definition. Indisputably, he can momentarily rescue the elements from becoming or dispersion, and actualize their mimetic power in *effectively* ordering them in the image of the Ideas, but he will never be able to guarantee this order that at no point will its internal structure or harmonious proportion cease to represent an Idea, if not by force of a promise. Were it ever to manifest itself, the risk of this final illusion would remain an inescapable death threat for the demiurge.

We now stand before a series of consequences that we must carefully clarify. The demiurge is not up to the task of perfecting the resemblance of the world to its model, neither in space nor in time.[2] In order that the world might have been able to *forever* escape the risk of such a dissolution, and thus such an illusion, it will have had to contain, within the productive principle of its genesis—as is the case for every element—the internal mimetic force that would allow it at any point or time to resemble the model of the Ideas. Of course, the soul of the world, in harmoniously regulating the economic equilibrium of its losses, will have ensured the world's perfect autonomy and an internal form of conservation; however, the principle of this animation would hinge on the demiurge's goodwill. But why then did the demiurge not inscribe—or could he not have inscribed—this representation into the organization of the world?[3] Why did he not make of its genesis the very principle of its conservation? And why must he necessarily relate the ideal form of this representation to the volitional acts of his own deliberation alone?

§2. There is thus a paradox upon which we wish to insist. On the one hand, if the demiurge can take hold of the elements to order a world in the image of the Ideas, it is *thanks* to the phenomenal predispositions and the mimetic potentialities of their very geneses.

---

2. Neither in space, since the demiurge's representation is limited to the already constituted or configured—and therefore already represented—structures of the elementary corpuscles, nor in time, since time itself will produce the mimetic structure of the representation of the world.

3. Regarding the question of whether this inscription was accomplished in the *Laws*, see note 19 of chapter 1 of the present study.

But, on the other hand, and *because of* such a genetic disposition, because of the irreducible losses proper to each element, the demiurge found himself incapable of providing this world with the indefectible means of resembling its model. It is thus one and the same thing that both *allows* the demiurge to organize the world, thus to be defined as an all-powerful god, and *prevents* him from making this world definitively indissoluble, thus presenting him as an inoperative and powerless god. From this mimetic paradox will ensue the demiurge's (noetic) predicament, and from such a predicament the world will have to content itself with living with the demiurge's *promises* as its sole warranty and statute.

After having both proclaimed the excellence of his product (the image of the world) and the impossibility of perfectly applying this product to its model (the ideality of the immortal gods), after having, let us say, perceived that this image, as beautiful as it may have been, could at any moment be reduced to vain illusions, the mimetic productive demiurge will be transformed into a promising demiurge. And, as we will see, this promise will constitute a sort of delegation, indeed a renunciation or abandonment, and perhaps even a sacrifice. Indeed, once the demiurge promises the world to never dissolve its bonds through an act of will, he both proclaims the necessity of completing the world's established order and the withdrawal of his own interventions. But how, then, if he henceforth refuses any involvement with the world, will he still be able to keep his promise?

This promise would commit the demiurge to never *will* the annihilation of the world. But this commitment, we argue, raises a double stakes, a double operation that will allow the demiurge not only to maintain, for a certain time, the representation of the world in the image of the Ideas, but above all to provide the world with the means of deploying, during this still indefinite time, the totality of the forms this model contains. According to the principle of the best of all possible worlds, while the world is already perfect in itself, it still lacks something—not something that would make it more harmonious, but something that would finally allow it to catch up with its model *to infinity*. It will be a matter for the demiurge, by means of a sort of spontaneous delegation, of continuing his building of the world through infinitely complicating all the possible relations of its constitution, in ultra-refining the elementary relations of its harmony to the point of making its most solid bonds untenable and inscribing a principle of dissolution into them—a principle that ought to *necessarily* lead each of the bodies thus organized toward a slow but certain death. This extreme refinement will constitute the formation of a human soul. And, as we will see, by inscribing this human soul into the soul of the world, and then inscribing an irreducibly mortal body of flesh into this human soul, thus in completing the world thorough a death principle—a sort of body-tomb in the memory of the immortal gods—the demiurge will be able to both keep his promise and experience the trial of his symbolic death.

The Birth of the Human Soul

The Demiurge's Promise

§1. Just as the demiurge's construction had to be conceived of in mimetic terms, this representation must be defined as an act of promising. What we above called the specifically productive function of the demiurge, his *material* production, consisted in forming a purely arithmetical relation of proportion between fire, air, water and earth. This entering into relation defined in 32*b* corresponds to the formal establishment of the regular polyhedrons or solids (the elementary bodies) and is effectuated through a systematic cutting out into determinate triangular surfaces (the nuclear particles). Then comes the *mimetic* production of the world; this is the insertion of an intelligent soul into the world, a geometrico-harmonious principle, a principle of autonomy, economy, and conservation that constitutes the double circular motion of the celestial sphere. This proportion, defined from 35*a* to 36*d*, is of a different order; it is invisible and issues neither from solids nor surfaces but from gaps of determinate lengths and distances (the planetary intervals). The third and final great step of the demiurge's production, after having been material and mimetic, will become *promissory*. The completion of the world will now consist not only in carrying out its production, in maintaining its representation on the threshold of an ideality, but furthermore, and henceforth especially so, in keeping a promise, that of never dissolving what has just been mimetically organized.

§2. Let us now attempt to situate this promise within the demiurgic production of the world. We revealed above a sort of temporal coincidence between the demiurge's noetic aim—his projections toward the nature of the model—and his effective action upon the sensible. This coincidence consisted of three specific points and thus described three logical but distinct conclusions. Let us schematically summarize these: (1) *in taking hold of* (παραλαβὼν) the material phenomena (30*a*) in order to assemble a world, the demiurge was able to insert an intelligent soul, or a principle of conservation into this world; (2) *in inserting* into the sensible body of the world (εἰς . . . αὐτοῦ . . . ἔτεινεν) (34*b*) the harmony of such an intelligence, he was able to mimetically organize the world as the starry heavens; and (3) it is *in thus organizing* (διακοσμῶν) the heavens (37*d*) that he was able to enumerate and make the intelligent soul of the world intelligible—whence, let us again note this, the *simultaneous* birth of the heavens and time (38*b*). In other words, if, on the one hand—according to the principle of the *anteriority* of the soul over the body—the building of the world presupposes the representation of the heavens, and if, on the other hand, this representation necessarily involves—according to the *numerical* principle of motion—the representation of time, then the production of the world *will have always already taken place* *"in"* time. But, in fact, a question thus poses itself: are the time of the enumeration of the world as heavens and the time of the production of the world as enumeration still the same time?

According to hypotheses of the phenomenological type, one could say that there are on the contrary two different times: an *originary* time and a *derivative* time.[4] One would correspond to

---

4. Therefore, differently from the Husserlian and Heideggerian theses on the two orders of time (the time of the phenomenal world and the retentional time of *absolute consciousness* [Husserl] or the time of *Dasein*'s existential extases [Heidegger]), what we would be attempting here to call "the time of originary expenditure" would be a time that would be irreducible to any genetic constitution of the phenomenon and any ontological project of *Dasein*'s. This time would not constitute the possibility of an egological order between phenomena or of an

the *phenomenal representation of the elements,* and the other to the *noetic representation of the world.* The latter would constitute the temporal order according to which the planetary motions of the heavens are enumerated (from daily cycles to the periods of the Perfect Year); this is the properly cosmic time—the time of the clepsydra, and of the clock. And the first will determine the temporal order according to which the genetic appearance of the elements is articulated—those the demiurge takes hold of to numerically represent the world as the starry heavens; it would thus be a matter of a pre-cosmic time, a time within which the remembrance of elementary genesis is related to and united with, in an indissoluble way, the anticipation of a determinate form. In other words, and still according to this hypothesis, the demiurge's first productive acts and the first moments of his taking hold of the phenomenal body of the sensible will constitute so many gestures predetermined by the temporal order of the phenomena. Each of them would in fact have always already been determined by the temporal order *according to which* the genesis of the elements (phenomenally) manifests itself to the demiurge's productive gaze. But if the building of the world presupposes the demiurgic representation of the heavens, then this representation will necessarily have to *coincide* with the numerical representation of time. What we above called the genetico-phenomenal representation of originary time would constitute the *possibility* of this coincidence and consequently the *possibility* that the demiurge produce *within* time a world determined *by* time.

Moreover, this pre-cosmic temporal order would itself determine the gap between representations. In fact, if the *taking-hold* the demiurge exerts on the phenomenal bodies of the elements was already determined by the time of their appearance, the aim of his noetic projection will never return to this side of its phenomenal aspect. If this taking-hold had indeed always already been subject to the linear becoming of the elements it apprehends, the demiurge would in fact be incapable of noetically perceiving

---

existential horizon between the extases, but would determine the possibility of a purely restorative formal configuration presupposed by any genetic or ontological constitution of temporality.

the distances or the temporal gaps that separate each of the momentary and singular phases constituting their own configuration. Being thus incapable of recovering the genetic losses owing to the temporal becoming of the elements in every case, and deprived of noetic means before his own apperception of the phenomena, the demiurge's representation will never be capable of entirely unbinding itself from the risk of a transcendental-type illusion. The resemblance of the world to the model will thus not be guaranteed in its principle, and the demiurge himself will find himself profoundly threatened in his ownmost authority.

§3. The demiurge will have to keep his promises in a very specific time and place. He will have to commit his word precisely where and when his noetico-practical taking-hold had always already in some way escaped him in time—in the time of the linear becoming of the genesis of the elements. However, there would be something both necessary and untenable or unkeepable [*intenable*] in this infinite promise that we must attempt to analyze.

As soon as the demiurge noticed that his world, as perfect as it may have been, could not in and of itself, through the (geometric and physical) productive laws of its constitution, avoid continuously suffering the genetico-temporal operation of its production, as soon as he understood that he was not up to the task of erasing the *threat* of such a risk of dissolution, and thus illusion from the world, he promised the world to do everything he could to allow it to catch up with its model *to infinity*.

As we will see in the following paragraphs, this promise will require that the demiurge both renounce his productive power, thus acquit himself from any responsibility with respect to the world, and introduce a principle of effective death within the organized whole of the world, a sort of sacrifice of which he would himself be both subject and object. It could therefore seem strange, indeed paradoxical, that immediately after having promised to preserve the bonds of the world, the demiurge would have chosen to withdraw his functions. According to our hypothesis, withdrawing from the world in order to give it death, or to put it to death, would be the properly demiurgic manner of keeping a promise. He would thereby transmit to the divine subaltern beings he just produced (the heavenly bodies) the power to create a specifically mortal race, a race whose death would have as its fate not only the annihilation of a body but first and foremost to constitute itself as the first and last *guarantor* of this promise. Through the intermediary of this delegation to his functionaries, the demiurge would transmit to mortals as much the care as the concern to make of their own death, or of their own sacrifice, the infinite promise of an immortality. This is why this race, human *par excellence*, will have to *learn*, to learn to educate itself, to speak, think, and philosophize. As the *Phaedo* says, to philosophize is to learn to die, and especially to die within immortality. It is thus learning to keep the demiurge's promise, to keep the promise of another, or to keep this promise in the place of an other and for an other. The demiurge will thus have to command that the world itself, unless benefiting from an internal economic principle of conservation, takes it upon itself to create a mortal race capable of philosophizing and honoring the immortal gods. He will have to command a sort of auto-sacrifice to the world, a relinquishing of its most restricted part to save the universality of its whole. This sacrifice will thus have the function of momentarily suspending the threat of dissolution—and illusion—from which the demiurgic representation of the world itself continuously suffers. Furthermore, short of being able to perfectly apply this world to its divine model, short of being able to make a perfect double (εἰκών) of it, the demiurge had the "promising" idea of making a *sanctuary* (ἄγαλμα) of the world in the memory and honor of the immortal gods.[5]

---

5. On the term *agalma* as a cult object, the reader will consult Hansjörg Bloesch, *Agalma: Kleinod, Weihgeschenk, Götterbild: Ein Beitrag zur Frühgriechischen Kultur- und Religionsgeschichte* (Bern: Benteli, 1943), especially 9–12 and 24–30 (cf. André Rivier, "Sur le rationalisme des premiers philosophes grecs," *Revue de Théologie et de Philosophie* 5, no. 1 [1955]: 6 n. 4). As Louis Gernet writes,

> there is a word that, in its widest use, implies the notion of value, it is the word *agalma*. It can be related to all kinds of objects—even, occasionally, to human beings as "precious." It most often expresses an idea of richness, but especially of a noble richness (horses are *agalmata*). And it is inseparable from another idea suggested by an etymology that remains visible therein: the verb *agallein* from which it is derived means both to adorn and to honor. . . . It is not irrelevant to add that at the classical age, it became fixed within the meaning of an offering to the Gods, especially of this type of offering represented by the statue of the divinity.

The Birth of the Human: Its Soul and Its Body

§1.

Prior to the coming to be of time, the universe had already been made to resemble in various respects the model in whose likeness the god was making it (ἀπείργαστο εἰς ὁμοιότητα ᾧπερ ἀπεικάζετο), but the resemblance still fell short (ταύτῃ ἔτι εἶχεν ἀνομοίως) in that it didn't yet contain (μήπω . . . περιειληφέναι) all the living things that were to have come to be within it. This remaining task (τὸ κατάλοιπον) he went on to perform, casting the world into the nature of its model (τὴν τοῦ παραδείγματος ἀποτυπούμενος φύσιν). (39e; PCW, 1243)

Once the demiurge's intellect fixated upon such a model, he discerned its particular properties (οἷαί τε ἔνεισι) and the number (καὶ ὅσται) of the Ideas (ἰδέας) its nature comprised in its essence (39e); he therefore did not perceive one idea alone or one species of living thing alone—this perfect species of the superlunary world—but four different species. Each of them will respectively correspond to the specific nature of an element: the heavenly species of the gods for fire, the winged species of birds for air, the aquatic species of fish for water, and finally for earth, any species capable of walking upon a firm ground, the human race among these.[6]

The demiurge will have created the nature of the (purely ignitive) heavenly bodies through and through. For the remainder, however, he will personally take on the production not of their entire soul but only the parts able to exercise the function of the

---

And this, he adds in a note,

> following a more aesthetic and "positive" conception, in contrast to another, Aegean of origin, that sees in the cultural statue the site of the "mystical" virtues; but not, incidentally, without the occasional irruption of the notion of a mysteriously living thing in the word *agalma*: we will find in this regard an interesting development on the basis of metaphor in Plato, *Laws*, XI, 930e. ("La notion mythique de la valeur en Grèce" [1948], in *Anthropologie de la Grèce antique* [Paris: Maspéro, 1968, reprint, 1982), 127 and n. 10)

Concerning the *Timaeus* in particular, the reader will consult Cornford, *Plato's Cosmology*, 99–101, and Brague, *Du temps chez Platon et Aristote*, 60.

6. *Timaeus*, 42b-c and 91d–92c (cf. Cornford, *Plato's Cosmology*, 142).

knowledge and worship of the gods, those parts that are thus immortal and in the grip of the economic cycles of metempsychosis. Just like the soul of the world, this specifically human part of the soul will remain indestructible as long as the demiurge represents its principle to himself in the image of the Ideas. With respect to the mortal part of the soul, including the body of flesh, the demiurge, as we have noted, will delegate or abandon (παρέδωκεν) (42*d*) his laboring power to the subordinate species of the gods he just engendered. While imposing upon them to follow the proportional principle of the production of the world, he will order them to produce the organic tissue of the mortal living thing, to inscribe into it or to graft upon it the immortal part of the soul and thus to realize a great number of individual units, each composed of a soul and a body.[7]

---

7. Cf. Paul Kucharski, "Eschatologie et connaissance dans le 'Timée,'" in *Aspects de la spéculation platonicienne* (Paris: Nauwelaerts, 1971), 317 et seq. And it is at this very moment that the soul will become mad.

And they went on to invest this body—into and out of which things were to flow—with the orbits of the immortal soul (τὰς τῆς ἀθανάτου ψυχῆς περιόδους). These orbits, now bound within a mighty river, neither mastered that river nor were mastered by it, but tossed it violently and were violently tossed by it. Consequently the living thing as a whole did indeed move, but it would proceed in a disorderly, random and irrational way that involved all six of the motions. It would go forwards and backwards, then back and forth to the right and the left, and upwards and downwards, wandering every which way in these six directions. For mighty as the nourishment-bearing billow was in its ebb and flow, mightier still was the turbulence produced by the disturbances caused by the things that struck against the living things. Such disturbances would occur when the body encountered and collided with external fire (i.e., fire other than the body's own) or for that matter with a hard lump of earth or with the flow of gliding waters, or when it was caught up by a surge of air-driven winds. The motions produced by all these encounters would then be conducted through the body to the soul, and strike against it. (That is no doubt why these motions as a group came afterwards to be called "sensations" [αἰσθήσεις], as they are still called today.) It was just then, at that very instant, that they produced a very long and intense commotion. They cooperated with the continually flowing channel to stir and violently shake the orbits of the soul. They completely bound that of the Same by flowing against it in the opposite direction, and held it fast just as it was beginning to go its way. And they further shook the orbit of the Different right through. . . . It is this very thing—and others like it—that had

§2. According to its purely ignitive form and its double circular motion (that of the same and that of the other), the celestial species of the heavenly-body-gods (which must not be confused with the ideal gods) shares with the body and soul of the world, of which it is an integral part, an economic principle of autarky and conservation.[8] Like the rest of the world, and as long as the

---

such a dramatic effect upon the revolutions of the soul. Whenever they encounter something outside of them characterizable as *same* or *different*, they will speak of it as "the same as" something, or as "different from" something else when the truth is just the opposite, so proving themselves to be misled and unintelligent (ψευδεῖς καὶ ἀνόητοι γεγόνασιν). Also, at this stage souls do not have a ruling orbit taking the lead. And so when certain sensations come in from outside and attack them, they sweep the soul's entire vessel along with them. It is then that these revolutions, however much in control they seem to be, are actually under their control. All these disturbances are no doubt the reason why even today and not only at the beginning, whenever a soul is bound within a mortal body, it at first lacks intelligence (κατ᾽ ἀρχάς τε ἄνους ψυχὴ γίγνεται τὸ πρῶτον). (*Timaeus*, 43a–44b; PCW, 1246–47)

On the two types of madness Plato speaks of, *primary madness*, madness (ἄνοια) caused by bodily conditions (*Timaeus*, 86b 2) or ignorance (86b 4), or *madness as a divine impulse*, the delirium (μανία) that makes us break with habits and customs (*Phaedrus*, 244a), the reader will consult Joubaud, *Le corps humain*, 178–92; Pierre-Maxime Schuhl, "La pathologie mentale selon Platon dans le *Timée*," in *Études sur la fabulation platonicienne* (Paris: Presses Universitaires de France, 1947), 116 et seq.; Yvon Brès, *La psychologie de Platon* (Paris: Presses Universitaires de France, 1968), 300–308; Luc Brisson, "Du bon usage du dérèglement," in *Divination et rationalité*, ed. Jean-Pierre Vernant et al. (Paris: Seuil, 1974), 236 et seq.; and C. Chiesa, "Socrate divin: Figures de la divination dans le *Phèdre*," in *Understanding the* Phaedrus: *Proceedings of the II. Symposium Platonicum*, ed. Livio Rosselli (Saint Augustine: Academia Verlag, 1992), 313–18.

8. There would thus be four categories of Θεῖος in the *Timaeus*: the purely *intelligible* divinity (the model of the immortal gods [41c, 42a, 90c]); the *artisan* divinity (the demiurge himself [47a]); the divine in the *cosmological* sense (this is the world composed of the fixed stars and the planets [36a, 40a, 40b, 42d, 44d, 68c, 80b]); and finally the properly psychological divinity (this is the soul of the world or the rational part of the human soul [44d, 44e, 69c, 69d, 72d, 73a, 73c, 76b, 85a, 88a]). For a detailed classification, see R. Mugnier, *Le sens du mot* ΘΕΙΟΣ *chez Platon* (Paris: Vrin, 1930), 116–17; Jean Van Camp and Paul Canart, *Le sens du mot* Θεῖος *chez Platon* (Louvain: Université de Louvain, 1956), 247–83; and Gilbert François, *Le polythéisme et l'emploi au singulier des mots* ΘΕΟΣ, ΔΑΙΜΩΝ *dans la littérature grecque d'Homère à Platon* (Paris: Les Belles Lettres, 1957), 246–305.

demiurge will make an ideal representation of it to himself, these gods will be exempt from aging and sickness. This immortal soul will thus be composed from the same elements and assembled according to the same proportions as those the demiurge made use of to produce the world. And this mixture, while it is nonetheless not as pure as the first (41*d*), will be divided by the demiurge in a krater and have its parts distributed in each heavenly body that covers the vault of the heavens. "Then he would sow each of the souls into that instrument of time suitable to it, where they were to acquire the nature of being the most god-fearing of living things (τὸ θεοσεβέστατον)"[9] (41*e*–42*a*; PCW, 1245).

Among the three other mortal species, one of them will have the privilege of honoring the ideal gods. This is the human race. It possesses a soul whose immortal form, we will see, will be able, through an act of veneration, to keep the demiurge's promise in his stead, the promise that the bonds that harmoniously weld the parts of the world will never be broken. However, regarding these three species, each as much as the other, the demiurge will neither be able to noetically represent them nor to produce them by his own hands, failing which they would become equal to the divine

---

9. "Now surely human life has something to do with the world of the soul, and man himself is the most god-fearing of all living creatures, isn't he (καὶ θεοσεβέστατον αὐτό ἐστι πάντων ζῴων ἄνθρωπος)?" (*Laws*, X, 902*b*; PCW, 1559). Likewise, in the *Protagoras*, "It is because humans had a share of the divine dispensation that they alone among animals worshipped the gods (ζῴων μόνον θεοὺς ἐνόμισεν), with whom they had a kind of kinship, and erected altars and sacred images (καὶ ἐπεχείρει βωμούς τε ἱδρύεσθαι καὶ ἀγάλματα θεῶν)" (322*a*; PCW, 757). Cf. Taylor, *A Commentary on Plato's* Timaeus, 259–60. Let us once again emphasize the use of the term *agalma* as a commemorative relation to the divine. With respect to this honoring of the gods, J. Rudhardt writes:

> Θεοσέβεια concerns the practice of certain customs, but it also describes, along with the respect of values, a notion closely related to those of truth and justice. Of rarer usage than εὐσέβεια, it is quite close to it, and can like it be opposed to ἀσέβεια, while having a smaller range, and in accordance with etymology of course defines the virtue both terms signify with respect to the gods.
>
> The name εὐσέβεια indeed signifies a quality, that of εὐσεβής, to which is opposed a contrary quality: ἀσέβεια or δυσσέβεια. One seeks the first, encourages it, lauds those who possess it, while avoiding the second, blaming the ἀσεβεῖς. Εὐσέβεια is thus a positive quality, as indicated by the

species of the heavenly bodies, and the world will not have contained within it all the possible forms of the living model.

It is you, then, who must turn yourselves to the task of fashioning (δημιουργίαν) these living things, as your nature allows. This will assure their mortality (θνητά), and this whole universe will really be a completed whole. Imitate the power I used in causing you to be (μιμούμενοι τὴν ἐμὴν δύναμιν περὶ τὴν ὑμετέραν γένεσιν). (41c; PCW, 1245)

Consequently, only a *divine product* will be able to compose the mortal principle of the soul. This progeny is both begotten and divine. On the one hand, it has received a demiurgic and divine power from its father that allows it to carry on with the production of the world. But, on the other hand, insofar as it is the product of its father, it will only be able to produce a species condemned to die. Of course, this divine product will imitate the demiurge's power; however, its elementary composition not having been self-constituted *within* its genesis, its representation will never be able to guarantee the continuous unity of the beings it engenders. And this is precisely why the demiurge's sons will not have the power

---

prefix εὐ, indeed a virtue. Isocrates classifies it beside the σωφροσύνη and the δικαιοσύνη amongst the ἀρεταί. It manifests itself according to behaviors suitable to the verb εὐσεβεῖν. These behaviors are relative to several objects of different natures.

The easiest to characterize are those of ritual conducts and are defined by the observance of the rules of worship; they concern the sacred customs or objects, the ἱερά. Some of these, without being rituals, are related to any reality one holds as ἱερός. . . .

All these behaviors proceed from a complex feeling of respect, where fear, admiration and love are mixed together and complete one another. One of Plato's texts (*Phaedrus*, 250e–251a) lets us see this: it describes the emotions inspired by the sight of a being full of beauty. The boorish οὐ σέβεται man wishes to possess and to enjoy this being; the wise man on the contrary, permeated with a feeling that makes him tremble, treats it as a god: ὡς θεὸν σέβεται, and wants to consecrate his offerings to it. We can also make out elsewhere an internal attitude of submission, but this submission is accompanied with confidence; it permits resolution as it makes your strength and grants you the highest hopes. (*Notions fondamentales de la pensée religieuse et actes constitutifs du culte dans la Grèce classique* [Paris, 1992 (1958)], 12–13, 16)

to spare the composition of the animal species from a slow but gradual dissolution.

The novelty of this new production through spontaneous delegation would consist of building a multiplicity of individual units, composed of a body and a soul, themselves capable of detaching the immortal part of their soul from their body, of naturally undoing the bonds that graft it to the flesh of their body so as to, with honor, *return* it to the divine principle of their begetting. We would thus have an economy that would symmetrically correspond to the economy of the energetic restitutions of the sensible world. Not only, as we will see, would this economy of the soul and metempsychosis be correlative to it, but moreover it is through this economy alone that the world, in its totality, will find the guarantee of the demiurge's promises.

§3. We will devote the remainder of this study to describing the psychic and somatic conditions of such an economy. Let us recall first of all that each human being has a body and a soul, itself divided between a mortal part and an immortal part. The supreme function of the soul, the only one, when all is said and done, that the demiurge represents is described by Plato as a *daimōn*, a divine spirit (δαίμονα θεὸν) (90a), a power among the most sacred,[10] endowed with an intellect (νοῦς) (71b, 90d), thought (διάνοια) (71c,

---

10. ἱερώτατου, *Timaeus*, 45a (cf. 90a). On the δαίμων, τὸ δαιμόνιον, in Plato, as an intermediary function between divine and mortal being, see the *Symposium*, 202e–203a; *Phaedo*, 107d, 108b. 113d; *Republic*, X, 617e, 620d–621b, *Cratylus*, 398c; *Statesman*, 271e, 274b, 274d; on the δαίμονες as spirits, see the *Laws*, VI, 701c, 713d, and 854b. Cf. François, *Le polythéisme*, 266 et seq.; Onians, *The Origins of European Thought*, 118–19; and Léon Robin, *La théorie platonicienne de l'amour* (Paris: Alcan, 1964), 111–14. Dodds writes:

In the *Timaeus*, where he is trying to reformulate his earlier vision of man's destiny in terms compatible with his later psychology and cosmology, we meet again the unitary soul of the *Phaedo*; and it is significant that Plato here applies to it the old religious term that Empedocles had used for the occult self—he calls it the daemon. In the *Timaeus*, however, it has another sort of soul or self "built on to it," "the mortal kind wherein are terrible and indispensable passions" (69c). Does not this mean that for Plato the human personality has virtually broken in two? Certainly it is not clear what bond unites or could unite an indestructible daemon resident in the human head with a set of irrational impulses housed in the chest or "tethered like a beast untamed" in the belly. (Dodds, "Plato, the

88c), reason or wisdom (φρόνησις) (71d, 75e), and finally with a power of deliberation (βούλησις) (70e, 71a). This immortal part of the soul will be situated in the head; the spherical form of the skull will allow a perfect revolution of the circle of the same and the other (44d), and its position at the outer extremity of the body will bring the human closer to the gods. It will provide it the means to spontaneously turn itself toward the site from where the divine principles of its birth issue (90a). From this elevated gaze, the human will have acquired the privilege of an upright and vertical stance (90b).[11]

As concerns the mortal part of the soul, entirely built by the divine heavenly bodies, it represents the irrational part of the human being; it is, according to the terms used in the *Republic*, a sort of wild and monstrous beast (IV, 439b), a being of passion, inexhaustibly desiring enjoyment and satisfaction (439d).[12] But this

---

Irrational Soul, and the Inherited Conglomerate," in *The Greeks and the Irrational*, 213–14)

11. *Timaeus* 90b. There would thus be a purposeful relation between the upright stance of the human and the cognitive function of the divine νοῦς (cf. Claude Gaudin, "Remarques sur la 'météorologie' chez Platon," in *Revue des Études Anciennes* 72, no. 3 [1970]: 338). Aristotle had strongly emphasized the theological reasons of what we could call the "fundamental anthropological law of uprightness":

In man the forelegs and forefeet are replaced by arms and by what we call hands. For of all animals man alone stands erect (Ὀρθὸν μὲν γάρ ἐστι μόνον τῶν ζῴων), in accordance with his god-like nature and substance (διὰ τὸ τὴν φύσιν αὐτοῦ καὶ τὴν οὐσίαν εἶναι θείαν). For it is the function of the god-like to think and to be wise; and no easy task were this under the burden of a heavy body, pressing down from above and obstructing by its weight the motions of the intellect and of the general sense. When, moreover, the weight and corporeal substance became excessive, the body must of necessity incline towards the ground. In such cases therefore nature, in order to give support to the body, has replaced the arms and hands by forefeet, and has thus converted the animal into a quadruped. For, as an animal that walks must of necessity have the two hinder feet, such an animal becomes a quadruped, its body inclining downwards in front from the weight which its soul cannot sustain. (*The Parts of Animals*, book IV, 686a–686b; ACW 1070–71; cf. 653a, 656a, 657c, 662b, 669b, 689a, and 690a)

12. Plato clarifies:

Now, would we assert that sometimes there are thirsty people who don't wish to drink?

soul has two distinct and hierarchically separated parts. First of all the one we call *courage* (θυμός) (*Timaeus*, 70b-c); this is the outer part of the mortal soul. It is represented, in the winged carriage of the *Phaedrus*, through the docile, beautiful, and good horse (246a-b). Its function is to directly act upon the passions of the heart, to appease them to the point that they rediscover the path of reason. The second part is defined as a sort of *desire* or *instinct* (ἐπιθυμία) (*Timaeus*, 70b, 90b); it is the appetitive soul in the proper sense, which must incessantly be fed and satiated (70d-e). For its part, the appetitive soul corresponds to the black and rebellious horse of the *Phaedrus*'s carriage. But, so as to not tarnish the purely divine function of the soul, the demiurge's sons implanted this irrational source within another part of the body. They placed it at the height of the chest, right at the middle of the thorax, which they divided, along its width, through the intermediary of a diaphragm: the external part for courage, and the internal part for desire (*Timaeus* 69e–70a). After having situated the three levels of the soul, the most difficult still remained to be done: to define and compose the mortal body, its sexuality, its carnal form, its organic tissue, and the hereditary structure of marrow where the continuous cycles of metempsychosis are articulated.

Certainly, it happens often to many people.

What, then, should one say about them? Isn't it that there is something in their soul, bidding them to drink, and something different, forbidding them to do so, that overrules the thing that bids?

I think so.

Doesn't that which forbids in such cases come into play—if it comes into play at all—as a result of rational calculation (ἐκ λογισμοῦ), while what drives and drags them to drink is a result of feelings and diseases (διὰ παθημάτων τε καὶ νοσημάτων παραγίγνεται)?

Apparently.

Hence it isn't unreasonable for us to claim that they are two, and different from one another. We'll call the part of the soul with which it calculates (ᾧ λογίζεται) the rational part (λογιστικὸν) and the part with which it lusts, hungers, thirsts, and gets excited by other appetites (περὶ τὰς ἄλλας ἐπιθυμίας ἐπτόηται) the irrational appetitive part (ἀλόγιστόν τε καὶ ἐπιθυμητικόν), companion of certain indulgences and pleasures (πληρώσεών τινων καὶ ἡδονῶν ἑταῖρον). (*Republic*, IV, 439c-d; PCW, 1071) (cf. Brice Parain, *Essai sur le logos platonicien* [Paris: Gallimard, 1969], 105–6).

§4. The body the *Timaeus* speaks of is a body of flesh, and this flesh contains a sort of macro-molecule, marrow, whose nature is not only sexuate (91*b*-*c*) but again endowed with a genetic potentiality of the hereditary type.[13] Besides the fact that this marrow is a finely ordered material substance, it constitutes a psycho-somatic articulation of a great complexity. It is within it that the immortal soul comes to *graft* itself to the body of flesh; it is thus within it that the structural bonds will be broken on the day of death, thus freeing the immortal motion of the soul, and it is within it, furthermore, that the economy of the genetic restitution of the thereby liberated souls will be organized. Marrow, surrounded by its bone and its flesh,[14] is thus endowed with an elaborate structure and a decisive function for the demiurgic completion of the world.

After having received their building power from the demiurge, the heavenly-body-gods will borrow from the world (ἀπὸ τοῦ κόσμου δανειζόμενοι), as one borrows a sum of money, portions of fire, air, water, and earth. One day, these borrowings will have to be returned (ἀποδοθησόμενα πάλιν) (42*e*–43*a*), element by element, molecule by molecule, and particle by particle. Not only one day, at the time of death, must everything be returned, but furthermore, everything will have to be returned with a premium, a sort of interest. It will not be a matter of providing a surplus of elements, which would make no sense, but of returning an immortal soul as a supplement. To appease the threats of dissolution from which the soul of the world serenely suffers, the heavenly-body-gods will indeed be responsible for returning to the world the immortal soul noetically represented by the demiurge.

But, before returning in more detail over this point of economy, let us examine how the demiurge's sons proceed.

[They] bonded together into a unity the parts they had taken (εἰς ταὐτὸν τὰ λαμβανόμενα συνεκόλλων), but not with those indis-

---

13. Cf. Mugler, *La physique de Platon*, 159–60.

14. For a precise description of the first elements of the animal body, from marrow to bone, from bone to flesh up to its numerous by-products—muscles, tendons, ligaments, skin, hair, etc.—the reader will consult Joubaud, *Le corps humain*, 48–63.

soluble bonds (οὐ τοῖς ἀλύτοις) by which they themselves were held together. Instead, they proceeded to fuse them together with copious rivets so small as to be invisible (διὰσμικρότητα ἀοράτοις πυκνοῖς γόμφοις), thereby making each body a unit made up of all the components.[15] (43a; PCW, 1246)

These bonds are endowed with a very specific articulatory function. They articulate a new relation of proportion between the four elements (42e–43a); moreover, they articulate the thread of the organic tissue of marrow, the joining of marrow to flesh, of flesh to the tendons and of the tendons to the nerves (73d), up to the formation of the sensible impression of the living thing itself (pleasure and pain);[16] they will finally articulate the connection between the unity of the body of flesh and its immortal soul[17] (73b).

These bonds will thus have the direct and indirect function of *maintaining* the unity of a living organism, from the smallest tissue to the individuality of an entire body. However, we nonetheless see these bonds dissolve and perish. They are indeed subject to wear and tear, aging as well as diseases. The reason for this necessary dissolution is an economic one, correlative to the economic reason of the restitutions of energy in the cosmos. The bonds that articulate the divine body and those that articulate the human body have in common the fact that both are *proportional* and *invisible*. The only thing that radically distinguishes these bodies

15. The smallness and indivisibility of these bonds would be relative to the invisibility of the world of the Ideas, the ἀόρατος τόπος, from where, precisely, their respective assemblages would issue (cf. *Timaeus*, 36e; *Phaedo*, 85e; *Sophist*, 247b). See on this subject Charles Mugler, "Le corps des dieux et l'organisme des hommes: À propos de *Timée* 43a," *Annales de la Faculté des Lettres et des Sciences Humanies de Nice* 2 (1967): 8–9.

16. On the genesis of sensible impression (*Timaeus*, 61d), the distinction between impression (πάθημα) and sensation (αἴσθησις), the distress that any impression provokes in the soul (43c), and the circular motion entailed by the passage from the impression to its representation (64b), the reader will consult Joubaud's detailed study, *Le corps humain*, 150–57. On pleasure and pain (ἡδονή καὶ λύπη) (64c–65b), always dependent upon a harmony and its dissolution (cf. *Phaedrus*, 60b-c; *Philebus*, 31d; and *Republic*, IX, 583b–585a), see Brès, *La psychologie de Platon*, 323 et seq.

17. Cf. Joubaud, *Le corps humain*, 129.

from one another is the *necessity* that animal tissue become undone, to distend, dissolve, and perish, while this dissolution is not necessary for the divine heavenly body. It is thus not a matter of distinguishing here between two *types* of constitution. In themselves, in the structure of their initial assemblage, the bonds of the divine body, having been begotten, will themselves one day become undone (41*b*). What distinguishes them from the bonds of the human body does not therefore rest upon a difference of nature—both are genetically and de facto essentially λυτοί—but upon two distinct economic forms of restitution. Once the demiurge's sons built the bodies of sublunary living things, they only undertook *borrowings*. Thus, the transaction of these borrowings will not pass between the demiurge and its progeny. The heavenly-body-gods indeed did not create the body of flesh, nor did they form the organic tissue of the living thing, in using a mixture of elements already organized by the demiurge and thus momentarily sheltered from all dissolution, but in directly intervening at the level of the nuclear particles of the elements. The demiurge having withdrawn his mimetic functions, the organization of this tissue will henceforth be destined to the systematic divisions of an eventual death.

Let us now attempt to clarify what one ought to call the *economic difference of restitution*. According to what has just been said, the distinction between the divine body and the human body does not issue from the constitutive nature of their respective bonds, which are in both cases invisible and dissoluble, but rests upon the type of *relation* the demiurge undertakes with respect to these bodies. On the one hand, for the divine body, the demiurge represents a perfect order in the image of the Ideas and promises to never interrupt the noetic aim of his representation. On the other hand, for the human body, the demiurge withdraws his mimetic power in delegating it to the heavenly-body-gods he just produced, thereby discharging himself from any *responsibility* with respect to the sublunary world (42*d-e*). The demiurge's first intervention thereby involves a restitutive economy of pure conservation. This economy, let us recall, is effectuated through a double movement. It presupposes, first of all, a perfect equilibrium between the centripetal laws of the Earth and the centrifugal laws of the radiance of the particles of fire. The dynamic equilibrium is thus continuous due to the simple fact that the heavenly bodies propagate the same quantity of fire that they received from the ascending movement of energetic restitution. On the other hand, this equilibrium, while perfect and continuous, will not be genetically, thus definitively maintained in the actuality of its own perfection. This cosmic exchange, indeed, will not last any "longer" than the *time* within which the demiurge will represent its order to himself in the image of the Ideas. However, we have seen that while the restitution of energies in the economy of cosmic conservation by mimetism is effective, that is to say quantitative (so many losses for so many gains), and while the ideal maintenance of this restitution is itself effective, that is to say continuously contained in an actual state of equilibrium, the risk of a dissolution, and thus, for the demiurge, of an illusion of the transcendental type or a symbolic death, remains an unavoidable threat—whence the necessity of engaging another economy.

This economy of dissolution is itself an economy of restitution. What distinguishes it from the first has less to do with its respective elements and properties than with the *strategic assemblage* they involve. There would not be on the one hand imperishable bodies and on the other hand bodies that perish. But since every begotten body is corruptible by definition, there would only be two ways of confronting the threatening burden of death, or, more precisely, two ways of *organizing* the strategy of an equilibrium of substitution between this threat of death and the desire for immortality: either through the continuous representation of a body in the image of an ideal model, or by the articulation of an organic tissue capable of both hosting an immortal soul and returning it to its place of origin.

Let us note for now that this articulation is economical and this economy is strategic. It is economic, first of all, in the sense that it will point for point return each of the elements that the world will have lent it. But, moreover, this economy presupposes a very specific strategy. For it does not organize this restitution with the mere goal of ensuring the energetic conservation of the world, but first and foremost with the aim of freeing the immortal soul from its body of flesh. Thus the elements will recover the circuit of the transformations of the Universe, and the soul will return toward the divine heavenly body to which it belongs by birth. And, since the immortal soul is the only thing in the human that the demiurge wished to represent, the world will thus have found, through this substitution or this new restitution, the guarantee that he, the living god, is ready to keep his promises. To put it schematically, the soul will be freed from the body in honoring the gods with its power of knowledge; on the basis of this emancipation, it will return to its heavenly body; and thanks to this restitution, the demiurge will remain good, thus always faithful to his promise. Things are not so simple and naive, of course. First of all, because the demiurge is no longer responsible for the fate of souls, no soul will be capable of *spontaneously*—as is the case for each element—returning to its place of origin. We will now see it deteriorate and fall once again into a body, thus incarnate itself and take on a new sex, or worse still, fall into an inferior species. According to a hierarchical principle, man will become woman and woman animal, and so on to the lowest degree of mortal living things. And the stronger this degradation will be, the more imminent the risk of a dissolution will be.[18] Additionally, this economic cycle of the restitution of souls directly depends upon the molecular tissue through which these souls graft themselves to the bone marrow of their bodies. The heavenly-body-gods have indeed composed, at the level of the elementary particles, a living tissue, marrow, capable not only of organizing the specifically hereditary distribution of the mortal kinds [*races*] from the bird to the human and from the human to the mollusk (91*b*–92*c*), but furthermore capable of structuring a specifically economical relation between two (divine) forces of the soul: the power to graft itself upon a body and the power to detach itself from it. In articulating the passage from this introduction to this evacuation, the organic tissue of marrow will allow the extreme perfection of the world to arrange a relation between a threat of death and the hope of immortality.

---

18. The increase of decrepitude will be determined according to the hierarchical level of the species: not according to the rapidity of decomposition or to the brevity of an organic equilibrium, but according to the imminence or the gradual growth of an eventual *risk of death*.

4

The Immortality of the Soul and Its Fate

The Molecular Structure of the Living Body

Marrow, between the Soul and the Body

§1. The formation of marrow (ἡ τοῦ μυελοῦ γένεσις) (73*b*) is a hereditary process, one allowing it both to set up the first elaborate substance of a body's organic tissue and to articulate the planning of the molecular schema of the body's organization. We will divide the development of marrow according to four correlative functions: (1) Marrow first of all *generates the framework of the living body*, from the bones to the joints, from flesh to tendons, nerves, ligaments and circulatory vessels. Its derivatives will be numerous and will be gradually ordered up to the outer parts and surfaces of the body in its totality; skin, fur, hair and nails.[1] (2) Moreover, the genesis of marrow will constitute a *stable specific difference between the animal kinds [races]*, not only between the three great classes of mortal living things (birds, mammals and fish), but further still between the diverse species of a same class (indeed the numerous families of a same species). (3) For every constituted species, the organizing principle of marrow will *ensure the fluidity and continuity of the physiological cycles of the living thing*. It will be a matter on the one hand of the double movement of respiration: exhalation-inhalation and, on the other hand, the nutritive circulation of the blood. (4) Through these ordered cycles, marrow will

---

1. On the skin, see *Timaeus*, 76*a*; on hair, 75*e*; on nails, 76*d*.

ultimately articulate a *link between the immortal soul and the body of flesh*: a bond that will allow the soul to graft itself upon the body and at the same time to separate itself from it.

For life's chains (οἱ γὰρ τοῦ βίου δεσμοί), as long as the soul remains bound (συνδουμένης) to the body, are bound within the marrow, giving roots (κατερρίζουν) for the mortal race. The marrow itself came to be out of other things. For the god [*sc.* the heavenly-body-gods] isolated from their respective kinds [*genre*] (ὁ θεὸς ἀπὸ τῶν ἑαυτῶν ἕκαστα γενῶν χωρὶς ἀποκρίνων) those primary triangles which were undistorted and smooth (ἀστραβῆ καὶ λεῖα) and hence, owing to their exactness (δι᾿ ἀκριβείας), were particularly well suited to make up fire, water, air and earth. He mixed them together in the right proportions (μειγνὺς δὲ ἀλλήλοις σύμμετρα), and from them made the marrow, a "universal seed" (πανσπερμίαν) contrived for every mortal kind [*espèce*]. (73b-c; PCW, 1274)

Let us note two essential points from this difficult passage, two points that will allow us to distinguish but also tie together the microscopic structure of marrow and the macroscopic assemblage of the Universe. Let us note, first of all, that the organic constitution of marrow is not realized on the basis of the primary schema of the elements, as is the sensible organization of the world. The heavenly-body-gods made direct use of the nuclear particles of the elements, the triangles. But they did not combine new regular polyhedrons with the help of these triangles, or even modify their specific schemas, but they assembled the logical relation between the polyhedrons differently. In the sensible world, the elements, forming distinct groups, mixed themselves together by way of *proportional analogy* (ἀναλογία). In marrow, conversely, the elements combine with one another according to a strict *symmetry* (συμμετρία).[2] Each triangle will no longer henceforth constitute

2. As Mugler writes:

However, a large number of macro-molecules of marrow precisely have the geometric property of being assignable to another figure formed like it, symmetrical to it in relation to a plane, but of the same nature as it. In the symmetrical position with respect to a plane, the two figures indeed seem to have different orientations, answering to the left-right opposition, but, by virtue of the regular structure of each polyhedron of which the

the determining unity of a *logical relation* between two or more polyhedrons, whatever they may be, but a *common limit* proper to two polyhedrons of different natures. Indeed, each lateral side of a triangle will have the function of joining back-to-back one surface of a fire tetrahedron, for example, with the surface of a same triangular structure of an air octahedron. The relation will thus be symmetrical and will only concern a single plane of the polyhedrons; their specific relation will thus be limited to the geometric properties of the triangles alone.

This combination will determine a second point of distinction between the structure of marrow and the universal order of the world. In the organic tissue of marrow, the polyhedrons will neither be mixed together, as in the gradual compression of the elements between terrestrial attraction and ignitive radiance, nor separated from one another, as in the continuous ascension of the return to the proper site of the elements. On the contrary, each of them will form a sort of *macro-molecule*,[3] a basic molecule characterized by a dominant polyhedron determining the specific element of an animal species. And, while the number of symmetrical combinations at the level of triangular surfaces is quite large—as large as the sum of the product of triangles of the same nature belonging to different polyhedrons—these types of molecular assemblages will nonetheless remain numerically finite. Thus each macro-molecule of marrow will constitute a basic structure corresponding to a determinate biological species (the air octahedron for the bird, the water icosahedron for the fish, and the earth cube for the mammal), but moreover each of these will define a relatively singular assemblage, corresponding to the varieties of each species just as much as to the families of each variety, indeed to the individuals of each family. This double molecular structure, between the two microscopic extremities of the animal kingdom—from generic speciation to the individualized varieties—will represent the hereditary function of marrow.

---

macro-molecule is composed, the two figures can be brought to coincide with one another. (*La physique de Platon*, 160)

Cf. Joubaud, *Le corps humain*, 56.

3. Following Mugler's term. See, among others, *La physique de Platon*, 159.

§2. Let us quote the rest of the text:

> Next, he implanted in the marrow (φυτεύων ἐν αὐτῷ) the various types of soul and bound them fast in it. And in making his initial distribution (κατ᾽ ἀρχάς), he proceeded immediately to divide the marrow into the number and kinds (τοσαῦτα καὶ τοιαῦτα) [*qualité et quantité*] of shapes (σχημάτων) that matched the number and kinds of shapes that the types of soul were to possess, type by type. (73*c*; PCW, 1274)

Thanks to marrow's speciating and differential structures, from the smallest organic tissue of an individual body to a determinate genus, the genetic character and biological organization determining the linearity of generations will be conserved upon the birth of a new body of flesh. Moreover, the sperm of every male sex, being a secretion of marrow (91*b*) deposited in the matrix of the female sex (91*d*), and the fruit of this procreation an embryo growing from this secretion, the macro-molecular structures of marrow will thus be defined as the genetic site of heredity.

While this hereditary structure distinguishes the marrow of bone and spine from every other organic and cosmological element in the Universe, once it was *organized at the molecular level* its physiological articulation would henceforth unfold according to the same physical laws as each of these elements. The autarky of the cosmos depends upon a continuous equilibrium between a heterogeneous force (from one element to its environment) and a homogeneous force (from one element to another). The same holds, *mutatis mutandis*, for the individuals of each species. On the one hand, each bird, human, or fish will be held in its natural environment by a force maintaining a certain geometric affinity between the dominant polyhedron of its molecular marrow and the polyhedrons determining the elementary nature of its environment.[4] But, on the other hand, each of these organized bodies will naturally have the tendency to associate, through the force of a gathering of like with like, with individuals of the same species

---

4. Cf. Mugler, *La physique de Platon*, 159–60.

(that is to say, of the same dominant polyhedron), whose specific assemblage and molecular combinations are closest to its own. But Plato assigns less importance to this biological determinism than it might seem. For the determination of this heredity is purely functional, and this function is subject to the economic cycle of the restitution of souls. Indeed, thanks to the genetic possibilities of molecular heredity, an immortal soul can be grafted upon a body of flesh. And this inscription depends on two things that must not be confused. First of all, according to the ascension of souls (from the slightest mollusk to the divine heavenly body) or their gradual decline (from the heavenly body to the oyster), each soul will have to direct itself toward one of the genera to which its specific *molecular type* belongs. This cycle of metempsychosis will thus be regulated by the proper heredity of the differential structures of marrow. But incidentally, this very inscription will depend upon the *genetic modalities* of molecular development for any individuation or any animation. It would be, in a sense, constituted by the properly circulatory modalities of the living thing, these modes according to which each macro-molecule of marrow can structure, in and from its genesis, the organic bond of the tissues and circulatory vessels where the physiological cycles of the living thing unfold: breathing and nutrition by blood. The restitutive economy of the dissolution of bodies must thus be situated at the lower level of the cosmos, between the *macro-molecular type* of marrow and the *physiological modalities* of its genesis.

The Physiological Circularity of the Living Organism

§1. The body lives according to the correlated laws of the dual process of respiration and the circulation of the blood. This dual closed circuit, acting in concert, has the task of nourishing of the body, of feeding and animating each of its parts, on the one hand by injecting oxygen molecules through the respiratory passages and the pores of the skin, and on the other hand by transforming the nourishment taken in into molecules of blood. This process, as a whole, is obviously of a great complexity. Furthermore, limiting ourselves to a merely schematic description, we will attempt to understand the mechanism through which—or more precisely through the *economy* of which—the immortal soul can both on the day of its birth bind itself to the body of flesh and at the hour of its death spontaneously abandon it. Let us briefly note that the demiurge's sons proceeded in two steps. They first of all *hollowed out canals in the body*, just like the channels and trenches one digs in gardens to irrigate the earth. They then planted two main canals around the spinal cord (the aorta and the inferior and superior vena cava), arranging the generative marrow between them (καὶ τὸν γόνιμον μεταξὺ λαβόντες μυελόν) to ensure the vigor, continuity, and regularity of circulation (77*d*).[5] The distribution of the circulatory vessels will begin from the heart (καρδία), situated at the height of the thorax, in the site of the θυμός (the irascible and mortal soul), out to the extremities of the limbs. The heart will have the task of tying together or centralizing the circuitry of the vessels, of producing blood (70*b*) and of warning the body of the dangers of stress it risks suffering.[6] Furthermore, to avoid the heart's excessive overheating in the throes of desires and passions, the heavenly-body-gods arranged at its sides a sort of safety valve, the lung (πνεύμων). This spongy organ has the ability to temper hot divine air (πνεῦμα), receive beverages, and thus to refresh the heart's overheating (70*c-d*)—whence the direct and continuous link between the circulation of the blood and the circuit of oxygen. After having hollowed out, distributed, and then arranged each of these canals, the gods still had to *prepare the irrigation* of these two circulatory passages (77*e*–78*a*). This is what we will now attempt to describe.

§2. While they operate in concert to ensure the body's survival and healthy equilibrium, these two physiological cycles take different paths and transport distinct elements. The respiratory passageways develop on the one hand through cutaneous tissue, the pores (79*d-e*), and are distributed in the form of a mesh

---

5. Cf. Cornford, *Plato's Cosmology*, 303–4; and Joubaud, *Le corps humain*, 66–68. One will also find in Diogenes of Apollonia's writings (DK, *B*6) an arrangement quite close to that developed in the *Timaeus* (cf. Laks, *Diogène d'Appolonie*, 61–64).

6. Cf. Joubaud, *Le corps humain*, 74 et seq.

throughout the body (78*b*). On the other hand, respiration is produced by the nasal cavity or the sinuses (79*c* and 79*e*), in this case passing through the pharynx to the lungs and back. The nutritive paths of the circulation of the blood for their part extend from the mouth to the same pharynx and from the pharynx to the digestive tube, ultimately to defecation. And even if these two circuits must be correlated at a certain point, their physiological mechanism (exhalation-inhalation and manducation-defecation) will remain distinct. Moreover, the elements that carry respiration—to wit, air and fire—will be smaller, finer, and lighter than those traversing the blood vessels—to wit, water and earth. And, in any case, no natural exchange could be tolerated without bringing about physiological troubles, upon which we will refrain from commenting.

Everything in the living tissue of the organism seems to begin with this enigmatic πηγήν πυρός (79*d*), this source of fire, this internal or interior fire, this inner heat that will have been situated in the left ventricle of the heart since the anatomical dissections of Philiston of Locri.[7] On the one hand, this ignitive source continuously heats the heart, and thus the entire body; it wears it out, tires it, and gradually dissolves every particle of its flesh. On the other hand, it tends to spontaneously escape the body to recover its natural site, the outer limit of the sphere. The mechanism of respiration would thus have a dual cause: one properly physiological, avoiding the excessive overheating of the heart and body; the other rigorously physical, the return to the proper place of the elements.

Let us now note that, for Plato, *to breathe* is first of all *to exhale* (ἐκπνοεῖν). Two principles control the mechanism of respiration. First of all, as we have seen, nature tends to reduce to its minimum, if not suppress, any void (κενός) brought about through a displacement of polyhedrons (78*b*). Next, the hot air (πνεῦμα) from respiration must move within us from the inside toward the outside (παρ᾽ἡμῶν ἔξω) (79*b*).[8] Furthermore, each time some

---

7. See on this subject Joseph Bidez and G. Leboucq, "Une anatomique antique du coeur humain: Philiston de Locres et le *Timée* de Platon," *Revue des Études Grecques* 57, no. 269 (1944): 27; and Joubaud, *Le corps humain,* 74–80.

8. In the *Cratylus* (399*d*), Plato, still quite close to Empedocles's theories on the ψυχικὸν πνεῦμα, will relate the ψυχή to the ἀναψῦχον, the power of heating

pneuma moves or is carried from one site to another (φέρεται), a certain internal void will be formed and a certain cooling will occur. To immediately fill this void and temper this caloric weakening, a sort of circular back-and-forth will have to unfold; such is the movement of *respiration*. When I exhale (some *pneuma*), I drive out the air adjacent to my nose and mouth, and the air thus repelled will in turn drive out the portion of air surrounding it—this will occur indefinitely. There would not yet be any external void, but an internal void that will need to be immediately filled in by borrowing a mass of air from the external world equivalent to the sum of the exhaled corpuscles of air; this is what Plato called *inhalation* (ἀναπνοή).

> And so inevitably the air, displaced all around (περιελαυνόμενον), enters the place from which the original air was breathed out (ὅθεν ἐξῆλθεν τὸ πνεῦμα) and refills that place, following hard on the breath. This takes place all at once (ἅμα), like the rotation of a wheel, because there is no such thing as a void. (79b-c; PCW, 1279)

Let us not thereby understand that I exhale *at the same time* I inhale, but that anytime some *pneuma* escapes my mouth and nostrils, no temporal gap can separate the interior void from the exterior void. There would not therefore be two successive movements of one and the same process, but two correlative and simultaneous processes of one and the same motion, the ignitive displacement of the pneuma. Just as I do not exhale at the same time I inhale, I do not inhale after having exhaled. According to the term ἅμα, it is indeed that I exhale *while* I inhale, but not in the sense of two continuous movements—which would come down to gradually suffocating the body. It would rather be a matter of two distinct processes acting in concert, that is to say, according to one and the same movement with a dual simultaneous trajectory. One could indeed say that exhaling is inhaling insofar as each time some amount of pneuma leaves my body, a parallel correlative process *immediately* produces, through nasal and cutaneous

---

and cooling the body (cf. Cornford, *Plato's Cosmology*, 307 n. 3). On the dual derivation of the verb ψύχω (I blow, I cool) into ψυχή (*anima*) and ψῦχος (*frigidus*), we will refer the reader to H. Ioannidi's article "Qu'est-ce que le psychisme?" *Filosophia* 15, no. 6 (1985): 286–87.

passages, an equivalent volume of air, thereby leaving no empty place nor any time for the formation of an empty space.

Both inside and outside, there can be neither void nor anything over-filled. But this equilibrium will only be assured for a brief amount of time, "for as long as the mortal living thing holds together" (78e; PCW, 1279)—in other words, so long as its *ignitive source* produces the pneuma its heart requires. It is indeed upon this ignitive source's continuous calorific regulation that the perfect circularity of respiration rests, the "neither void nor over-filled" respectively corresponding to a "neither too cold nor too hot."[9] According to the physical principles of the transformation of the elements, the internal air octahedrons enter into contact with the tetrahedrons produced by the ignitive source; these tetrahedrons divide the octahedrons into parts, thus creating this mixture of air and fire that is the pneuma. And since these particles of hot air contain a portion of fire, they will spontaneously tend to recover their natural site, situated at the outermost extremity of the sphere[10]—whence the need for continuous exhalation, an exit outside of the body either by the cutaneous, nasal, or oral passages. And since this pneuma also contains some amount of air, it will cool down when it reaches the outer environment, and the tetrahedrons will once again separate themselves from the octahedrons, each thereby recovering their respective place; the fire particles will escape from air toward the top, and the air particles, now free, will remain in their corresponding environment. This cooled air will serve to fill the exterior void caused by the continuous displacement of surrounding air just as well as fill the interior void caused by the expulsion of pneuma.

§3. However, the calorific cycle of respiration will not find its end in the closing of its circuit. The pneuma's cyclical motion not

---

9. The reader will also find this thermal equilibrium in Aristotle's biology. It is indeed on the basis of a measurable caloric distinction, two degrees of the body's concoction, that Aristotle will establish a specific sexual difference, man being *naturally* warmer than woman (*Generation of Animals*, I, 19, 726a; I, 21, 730a; IV, 1, 765b).

10. Cf. Charles Mugler, "Alcméon et les cycles physiologiques de Platon," *Revue des Études Grecques* 71, no. 334 (1958): 45.

only has the task of tempering, regulating, and equalizing the internal iginitive source, but also, and especially so, of recharging its continuous expenditures. Ultimately, everything would lead us to believe that, for the human, to breathe is also to nourish oneself. Indeed, Plato would not have failed to emphasize this. Once the interior fire follows the movement of the ejection of pneuma to which it belongs as a tetrahedron, all the while involving an immediate return of octahedrons, it brings with it cubes and icosahedrons, solid and liquid elements (78e), digested remains of food and drink, that it divides and decomposes into parcels, recomposes in the thick and reddish form of blood (αἷμα), and then carries and distributes within the vessels of circulation (79a).[11] Furthermore, each time the human breathes, each time that in exhaling pneuma its heart is cooled with surrounding air, this heart produces blood, and blood as nourishment, half-liquid half-solid, repairs the organism's wear and tear in spontaneously directing itself toward the parts of flesh, here liquid there solid, threatened with alteration.

Thus the two circuits of respiration would be united through one and the same ignitive source, an inner source whose physiological function would obey the same laws of attraction as the entire Universe (81a-b). But, unlike the cosmos, which for its part is protected by the demiurge's noetic gaze and indefinitely (which does not mean definitively) stabilized in an actual state of equilibrium, the continuous revolution of these cycles would only be maintained in a stable state for a brief amount of time, precisely as long as an organism's freshness and vivacity will last. According to Alcmaeon of Croton, to whom Plato implicitly refers, one day the human soul will no longer be capable of making the beginning of a new revolution out of the moment that imposes a term on the cycle of revolution.[12] The loop no longer being infinite, the

---

11. Cf. *Timaeus*, 80d and 81a. See also Cornford, *Plato's Cosmology*, 327; and Joubaud, *Le corps humain*, 80–82.

12. "In every case, whenever there is more leaving a body than flowing in [to replenish it] (Ὅταν μὲν δὴ πλέον τοῦ ἐπιρρέοντος ἀπίῃ), it diminishes (φθίνει πᾶν); whenever less, the body grows (ὅταν δὲ ἔλαττον αὐξάνεται)" (81b; PCW, 1281). Alcmaeon of Croton proposed two distinct physiological phases for the circulation of blood: ἀναχώρησις and διάχυσις. Once the first stopped reviving

exhaled pneuma will no longer coincide with the inhalation of cooled air, exhalation will be painful, fire will have difficulty transforming the elements into molecules of blood, the entire body, increasingly famished, will weaken, tire, age, and find itself condemned to die. But, this process of death is also a decomposition and a development, the systematic division into primary triangles and the simultaneous liberation of an immortal soul. It is this process of death that we must now define.

Death in the Soul of the Immortal Living Thing

Milk, Marrow, and Death

§1. There would come a point, in the organization of the universe, where the end of a cycle would no longer immediately coincide with the beginning of another. And this is the certainty of death; it is the guarantee that death will one day occur. But what exactly happens when the cosmic curve is broken? How does this interruption come about, and where in the body does it produce its effect? Nothing is more paradoxical than this instant of death; it causes the body to perish, decompose, dissolve, liquefy, and also frees its soul, liberates it so as to make it immortal. More precisely, it puts the body to death not to spare its soul from nothingness but with the single goal—through this soul—of saving and thus fulfilling the promise the demiurge will have committed to the world. The soul of the dead being is a promised soul; it must die so that the body of the world can be indefinitely represented through the demiurge's gaze.

Just as the genesis of the body of flesh for Plato is located at the elementary level of the particles, death has its place of origin in the primary schema of the particles. Death would be a continuous

---

the second, the beginning of a new cycle could no longer directly meet the end of another cycle; human life would exhaust itself, and the human would die (ἀναχωρήσει τοῦ αἵματος εἰς τὰς αἱμόρρους φλέβας ὕπνου γίνεσθαί φησι, τὴν δὲ ἐξέγερσιν διάχυσιν, τὴν δὲ παντελῆ ἀναχώρησιν θάνατον) (Alcmaeon of Croton, DK, *24 A 18*). As Vernant writes regarding this fragment, "In allowing the end to meet the beginning, the exercise of memory becomes the conquest of salvation, deliverance from becoming and death" (*Mythe et pensée chez les Grecs*, 97).

decomposition symmetrically opposed to the organic composition of the body, a sort of systematic de-schematization at the triangular level of marrow. As long as these triangles are new, young, and still fresh, as long as newborn marrow is *nourished with milk* (τεθραρμμένης δὲ ἐν γάλακτι) (81*c*), its consistency will remain tender, humid, vigorous; it will be continually vivified and thus still capable of confronting the triangles issuing from the external world, these half-solid half-liquid triangles, these forms of nourishment and drink that surround and uninterruptedly pester it. As long as this marrow is *milked*, its own triangles will keep a rigorous angle and a taut edge; they will be able to divide, master, and appropriate the particles attacking it through direct incorporation (81*c-d*), and the world will become nourishment. But this nourishment, if one can say so, is double-edged. On the one hand, it nourishes the body by serving as an element in the production of the blood, but on the other hand, its inexhaustible aggression against the body will end up ruining the latter. No longer being able to continuously struggle, the body will become so weak that it will find itself divided, decomposed, and eaten by the world. The end of its nutritive cycle will no longer constitute the beginning of another cycle, and it will die.

But when the roots of the triangles are slackened (ἡ ῥίζα τῶν τριγώνων χαλᾷ) as a result of numerous conflicts they have waged against numerous adversaries over a long period of time (ἐν πολλῷ χρόνῳ), they are no longer able to cut up the entering food-triangles into conformity with themselves (τὰ μὲν τῆς τροφῆς εἰσιόντα οὐκέτι δύναται τέμνειν εἰς ὁμοιότητα ἑαυτοῖς). They are themselves handily destroyed by the invaders from outside (ὑπὸ τῶν ἔξωθεν).[13] (81*c-d*; PCW, 1288)

13. Let us note here a particular difference in decomposition. On the one hand is a decomposition of the triangle's lateral sides through crumbling, grinding, or breaking (καταθραύω) (*Timaeus*, 56*e*; cf. 57*b*); in this case, the triangle is practically digested or assimilated by the dominant polyhedron. This is the passage from water to air or air to fire. And on the other hand is a decomposition through division (διαίρεσις) or dissolution (διάλυσις) (81*c-d*). It is a matter here of an interfacial tearing produced at the level of the root of the polyhedrons. It is a radical cut without return, without the possibility of reappropriating the elements through successive transformation (cf. E. M. Bruins, "La chimie du Timée,"

For the human there would thus be only one alternative: either it will eat the world or it will be eaten by the world. But the human cannot continuously master such an assimilation. The appropriation of the elements of the world will only last for a time, as long as the marrow of the body is nourished with milk, regenerated, and vivified.[14] There would thus be a directly constitutive link between the lactation of marrow and the lateral tension of the triangles in the human body. Should this milk lack purity, should it no longer regularly and constantly irrigate the fatty matter of marrow, the *edge* of the triangles joined back-to-back, surface against surface, would no longer be able to conserve the *rectitude* of its line. The line will no longer be absolutely *straight*, thereby bringing about a sort of air bubble between the triangles, a certain *minimal void* between the lateral surfaces of the polyhedrons. We would thus have a continuous and gradual formation of internuclear interstices, a distension internal to the polyhedrons that both unbinds the juxtaposition of the edges and shifts the symmetry of the surfaces; the geometrical order would thus be undone at its root and the organization of the body literally decomposed.

The *root* (ἡ ῥίζα) of the polyhedrons would constitute the internal *tension* of the lateral edges of the triangles. But, to maintain this tension, this force of combat, this vivacity of surviving, it needs milk. It must be nourished with milk to be strong, to be *able* to incorporate, assimilate, and eat the world. There would thus be a sort of elixir in this milk, a spermal liquid of immortality directly linked to the separation of the fleshes and the liberation of the soul.[15] As Plato writes,

---

280). On the term ῥίζα (rhizome, layer, cutting), see Archer-Hind, *The Timaeus of Plato*, 306; Taylor, *A Commentary on Plato's Timaeus*, 585–86; Cornford, *Plato's Cosmology*, 329; and Brague, "La cosmologie finale du *Sophiste*," 274–75.

14. "This is true of the species as a whole, and also of its individual members, each of which is born with its allotted span of life (καθ᾽ αὑτὸ τὸ ζῷον εἱμαρμένον ἕκαστον ἔχον τὸν βίον φύεται), barring unavoidable accidents. This is because its triangles are so made up, right from the beginning, as to have the capacity to hold up for a limited time (κατ ἀρχὰς ἑκάστου δύναμιν ἔχοντα συνίσταται μέχρι τινὸς χρόνου δυνατὰ ἐξαρκεῖν) beyond which life cannot be prolonged any further" (*Timaeus*, 89b-c; PCW, 1288).

15. One finds in the Homeric hymns an explicit substitution between the substance of marrow and the lively force of the αἰών. "Then he probed with a gouge

131

eventually (Τέλος δέ) the interlocking bonds (δεσμοὶ) of the triangles around the marrow can no longer hold on, and come apart under stress (τῷ πόνῳ διιστάμενοι), and when this happens they let the bonds of the soul go (μεθιᾶσιν τοὺς τῆς ψυχῆς αὖ δεσμούς). The soul is then released in a natural way (ἡ δὲ λυθεῖσα κατὰ φύσιν), and finds it pleasant to take flight (μεθ᾽ ἡδονῆς ἐξέπτατο). (81d; PCW, 1281)

From the de-lactation of marrow would thus issue the distension of the triangles, and from this distension the releasing of the soul. However, if it is necessary to distend the root of the triangles to free the soul from the body, and if it is necessary to de-lactate marrow to distend its root, the internal mechanism of de-lactation will constitute both a process of death and the first elaboration of an immortality. To de-lactate the body, to withdraw all force of incorporation from the body, is both, we will see, to let the body be a body, be a dead body, and to make of the body thus left dead a tomb to the memory of the immortal gods.

§2. This de-lactation indeed constitutes an opposite process: a decrepitude symmetrically opposite to the generation of bodies, a sort of internal counter-genesis that both makes an organism's development possible and inevitably leads this organism to the point of decomposition. According to the process of natural growth, the generation of the body of flesh issues from *blood*, this residue from nourishment. Through spontaneous auto-division, the elaborated matter of blood separates its properly liquid components from the more consistent components of fiber (ἰνός). In coagulating, this liquid will produce flesh, and the fibers will constitute sinews. Then, from this sanguine product, flesh-sinew, will issue a "sticky and oily" element, a sort of glue, a nourishing synovial liquid, allowing both the adherence of flesh to bone and the regular growth

---

of gray iron and scooped out the marrow [of life] (αἰὼν ἐξετόρησεν) of the hill tortoise." "Hymn 4b: Hermes Invents the Lyre," in *Anthology of Classical Myth: Primary Sources in Translation*, ed. and trans. Stephen M. Trzaskoma, R. Scott Smith, and Stephen Brunet (Indianapolis: Hackett, 2004); see also line 119 of this hymn and Pindar's *Hyporchemata*, 5. On this subject, the reader will consult Benveniste's article "Expressions indo-européennes de l'éternité," 109 (cf. Onians, *The Origins of European Thought*, 206).

of bone-matter[16] (82c-d). However, in order that this glue might prevent any outpouring of synovia, any unbinding of the flesh, any lateral displacement of the contracted muscle, it is necessary that the bone be regularly and continuously irrigated in its marrow. The adhesion of flesh to bone indeed depends on this irrigation. The process of death would thus have its source at this precise point in generation. For if death, as we have seen, issues from the separation of fleshes, and if this unbinding directly issues from poor irrigation, the drying out of marrow will necessarily constitute the biological origin of death. Regarding this irrigation, Plato speaks of a liquid whose purity knows no equal: "the purest (καθαρώτατον), smoothest (λειότατον) and oiliest (λιπαρώτατον) kind [espèce] (γένος) of triangles, forms droplets inside the bone (λειβόμενον ἀπὸ τῶν ὀστῶν καὶ στάζον) and waters the marrow (ἄρδει τὸν μυελόν)" (82d-e; PCW, 1282). The link between this sacred liquid[17] and the spermal substance of milk is obvious.[18] Thus described and situated in the process of generation, this spermolactation will allow the maintenance of the oleaginous state of marrow in its firmest state—and thereby allow the substance of the bones to remain sufficiently compact for the adhesion of the fleshes—and at the same time provide its own triangles with a rigorously taut root and well-sharpened edges.

But what exactly is at stake in this lack of lactation? The process of decrepitude will not have awaited the integral drying-out of marrow to put the body of flesh to death. The first germs of death do not come about when milk no longer flows, but rather when this flowing no longer occurs *drop by drop*—or, more precisely, when the *sequence* determining the gap between the drops is no longer regular. This sequence, no longer regulated on the principle of a clock (or, which comes down to the same, represented by the demiurge's noetic aim), will not be able to indefinitely prevent a

---

16. Cf. Joubaud, *Le corps humain*, 84.

17. "Seeing that it is a disease of the sacred part of our constitution, it is entirely just that it should be called the 'sacred' disease (i.e., epilepsy) (νόσημα δὲ ἱερᾶς ὂν φύσεως ἐνδικώτατα ἱερὸν λέγεται)" (*Timaeus*, 85b; PCW, 1284).

18. We will find such an assimilation in Aristotle's biology. In *Generation of Animals*, sperm will indeed act upon menstrual blood in the same way that the sap of the fig tree or pressure can make milk curdle (I, 20, 729a and II, 3, 737a).

brief gap of time from occurring between one drop and another, a sort of instant between the drops, a moment without drop, without milk and without life. It is an instant of death between the drops of life that deregulates the biological cycle of lactation—and thus of generation—from within. Each time such an instant occurs, the end of a drop will no longer be able to *immediately* coincide with the beginning of another drop. Marrow will dry out, bones will have the tendency to wear out, and fleshes to unbind. Physiological cycles will thus be disturbed in their very principle. For if the spermo-lactation of marrow becomes irregular, if the gap between the drops comes to create nuclear voids between the surfaces of the triangles, a disturbance through the production of interstices will necessarily take place inside the cycle of nutrition. The exhaled pneuma will no longer immediately and perfectly coincide with the inhalation of cooled air, exhalation will thus be progressively delayed, fire particles will no longer be able to systematically transform the elements into molecules of blood, nor thereby assimilate the world to the nutritive substances of food, and the body in its totality will be increasingly famished, tired, worn; it will age, then it will die. Everything, however, would lead us to believe that this gradual irregularity between the drops is a process internal to the very flowing of lactation. And while this process may be the reverse of that of generation, its form is nonetheless inherent to any generation, assimilation, and incorporation. It would produce momentary, discontinuous, and discrete phases of disincorporation inside the continuous outpouring of the spermal substance of milk. It would be in a sense a question of an internal force of disappropriation, a quasi-instantaneous development consisting of disincorporating flesh, separating it from its bone, to disincarnate the soul, free it from its body, to the point of reducing it to the purest degree of its immortality.

This force of disappropriation would be at the source of any decomposition, and thus at the origin of death. However, it is necessary to clarify that there is nothing strictly negative here. While the outpouring of milk-sperm into marrow is no longer regularly determined, the process of death would not directly issue from a *lack* of milk but from the *empty instants* produced within the outpouring of milk. There will always be enough milk, but this milk will be increasingly mixed with non-milk, empty air pockets that make the *absolute* appropriation and assimilation of the world by the body of flesh impossible. Death would thus not be the strict opposite of life or lactation; on the contrary, it would draw its origin from the disappropriating force of lactation. It is this force that we must now attempt to describe, asking ourselves what is its principle, its economy, and its implicit relation to the immortality of the soul.

From Sacrifice to Immortality

§1. The process of death through internal disappropriation involves a dual operation. The first is purely *biological*: it concerns physiological deregulation and the separation of the fleshes. The second is *cosmological*: it determines the liberation of the soul and the cycles of metempsychosis. There would thus be a sort of *layering* between these two operations—not a dependency of the causal type, but a displacement of functions, a substitutive and systematic relay from one to the other. It will of course be necessary that the bonds of flesh become distended so that the soul may withdraw from its body. The flight of the soul will represent the immediate effect of death. However, this liberation will not be the result of death. The biological operation of a putting to death of the body of flesh does not have as its goal or function the salvation of a soul, but rather the substitution of an economy of the restitution of souls for the economy of the conservation of the world; this is the properly cosmological operation of death.

As we have already noted, this second economy is strategic. For its part, it not only has the task of maintaining a certain equilibrium of the cosmos but must moreover ensure in its own way what the economy of conservation, constituted by the demiurge's representation, could not guarantee in principle. In other words, this strategy will operate in such a way that the putting to death of the body of flesh has as its sole task not only to simply preserve a soul but to make of this liberated soul the final guarantor of the demiurge's representations, and thus to substitute itself for his own representation. While this is very problematic, there would be a direct link between, on the one hand, the fact that the demiurge has withdrawn his mimetic power from the world and, in leaving, withdrawn any responsibility toward the body of the human—that he let this body become consumed in the rhythm of its own expenditures and irreducible temporal losses—and, on the other hand, the fact that he can only maintain the mimetic equilibrium of the world in the form of a promise. The incapacity the demiurge experiences to perfectly represent the ideal model of the gods, this powerlessness that should commit him to keep a promise toward the world, obligates him to abandon a part of the cosmos, to *sacrifice* it, to no longer make a representation of it to himself, and thus to let its body be reduced to the most absolute state of dissolution.

The economy of the restitution of souls would thus have as its substitute the operation of a sacrifice, a biological and cosmic putting to death that we must now clarify. It will always be a matter of economy, since the ultimate goal of metempsychosis will be to conserve cosmic equilibrium in its totality (and not only the equilibrium of the supra-lunary world). But this new economy will not have as its task ensuring the constancy of an actual state of equilibrium in maintaining a mimetic relation between the proportional bonds of the (sensible-intelligible) world and the numerical structure of the ideal model (the immortal gods). Its specific function must act directly upon the *maintenance* of the mimetic relation: not to realize this relation, but to guarantee the survival of this relation. The demiurge will have promised the world to never dissolve the bonds constituting it, bonds that represent it in the image of the Ideas. If this promise should one day be broken, the world in its totality would be irreversibly led toward death sooner rather than later. But how to guarantee such a promise? Does this question not bring the (poietico-mimetic) authority of the demiurge to its limits, thus to the threshold of his mortality and his own finitude? However, since he did not create the constitutive elements of the world through and through, when he promises to represent the order and harmony of these elements in the image of the Ideas he cannot proclaim himself the guarantor of this promise—whence his state of powerlessness and inoperativity. But, incidentally, and consequently, this question no longer concerns him; the fate of the world is no longer dependent upon his will and responsibility. The demiurge would thus be forced to appeal to a wholly other instance, an order that will have to take the commitment of his promises upon itself. And this is precisely where the sacrificial operation of the restitution of souls comes about.

According to our hypothesis, the commitment of this promise will be directly linked to an act of sacrifice. To guarantee such a promise, and thus to ultimately maintain the equilibrium of the cosmos, it is indeed necessary to put a part of the cosmos (the sublunary world) to death. One must introduce a process of death into this cosmos, one just as capable of decomposing a determinate part of it as it is of protecting its totality from an implicit dissolution. But how can such a small part of the cosmos spare the whole of the cosmos; how can it guarantee with its death that the entire Universe be truly and constantly the whole?[19] And what could it mean, in this case, to *sacrifice* a part, what does it mean to *save* the whole? Finally, what will happen to the demiurge if the sacrificed part does not manage to save the whole?

§2. This sacrifice has a very specific sense. It is indeed necessary that the part of the cosmos abandoned by the demiurge—this sacrificed part or body of flesh, non-represented and delivered over to the irreducible and disappropriating expenditures of time— become through dying *nourishment* (τροφή) for the whole of the cosmos. It must be a very specific nourishment, however, a sort of food both bound to the cosmic order and nonetheless dependent upon the body's biological nourishment: *milk*. However, any putting to death of the body would not *de facto* entail the creation of such a nourishment. It is not sufficient to *die*; one must also *die well*. In dying, in sacrificing oneself, the body of flesh will have to decompose *in such a way* that its liberated soul might serve as a nourishment for the demiurge's representations. The manner in which the body will die will consequently determine the manner in which the soul will free itself from it. In this sense, the liberation

---

19. There would thus be two types of economies of restitution. The first would concern the world's cosmic equilibrium (so many losses for so many excesses) and the second the world's "psychic" equilibrium. This equilibrium would not have as its task the regulation of the quantities of energies and the order of expenditures, but rather the commitment of a sacrifice capable of substituting the discontinuous return of an immortal soul for any continuous expenditure of energy.

of this soul will constitute a nutritive quality that is more or less good, more or less capable of maintaining the demiurge's representations and promises in a good state and in good shape. As Plato writes,

> keeping well-ordered the guiding spirit that lives within him [the human] (εὖ κεκοσμημένον τὸν δαίμονα σύνοικον ἐν αὑτῷ), he must indeed be supremely happy (εὐδαίμονα). Now there is but one way to care for anything, and that is to provide for it the nourishment and the motions that are proper to it (τὰς οἰκείας ἑκάστῳ τροφὰς καὶ κινήσεις ἀποδιδόναι). And the motions that have an affinity to the divine part within us are the thoughts and revolutions (διανοήσεις καὶ περιφοραί) of the universe.[20] (90c-d; PCW, 1289)

Concerning this soul-nourishment, two questions might be posed. The first concerns the properly cosmic and psychic operation of death: how must the body decompose so that the soul becomes nourishment, a celestial food, a beverage of immortality capable of keeping the demiurge up to the task of keeping his promises? The soul, the only part of the human that the demiurge will have willed to represent in the image of the Ideas, will now be defined as a *thought* (διανόησις). But not just any thought: it will be a thought of the model of the immortal gods, or of the sacred demon (δαίμων) placed within it by the demiurge in the form of a representation. It will think of these gods in both senses of the term: it thinks about the fact that the demiurge represents it in the image of the gods, but also about the fact that it has these gods themselves as the content of its thinking. In other words, in order that the soul might become nourishment, and thus so that it becomes immortal in letting itself be devoured by the ideal gods, it

---

20. On the link between εὐδαιμονία and δαίμων, we can refer to Heraclitus's *Fragment 119*: "The character of man is his guardian spirit (ἦθος ἀνθρώπῳ δαίμων)" (DK, *B 119*; TEGP, *135*, 174–75), or more specifically to Democritus's *Fragment 171*: "Happiness (εὐδαιμονίη) does not dwell in herds or in gold; soul is the dwelling of the guardian spirit (ψυχὴ οἰκητήριον δαίμονος)" (DK, *B 171*; TEGP, *207*, 636–37). Taylor, *A Commentary on Plato's Timaeus*, 634; Cornford, *Plato's Cosmology*, 354; Festugière, *Contemplation et vie contemplative chez Platon* (Paris: Vrin, 1978), 271; and Hadot, "Physique et poésie dans le Timée de Platon," 115.

will have to *come down to* the object of its own thinking.[21] There would no longer be any difference between cogitated content, the *cogitatum* (the fact that it is represented by the demiurge in the image of the gods), and the act of cogitation, the *cogitatio* (the fact it thinks of these gods):

> We should redirect the revolutions in our heads that were thrown off course at our birth, by coming to learn the harmonies and revolutions of the universe, and so bring into conformity with its objects our faculty of understanding, as it was in its original condition (κατὰ τὴν ἀρχαίαν φύσιν). And when this conformity is complete, we shall have achieved our goal: that most excellent life (τέλος . . . ἀρίστου βίου) offered to humankind by the gods, both now and forevermore.[22] (90d; PCW, 1289)

The second question will more directly concern the biological operation of death. What relation does the soul-nourishment undertake with the lactation of the body? Between the nutritive function of the body and that of the soul, between the lactation of milk-sperm and the cogitation of thoughts, there is a very tight link, a concurrence of an absolute rigor, an ultimate stake that would allow the sacrificed body to guarantee and ensure the demiurge's commitment toward the rest of the cosmos. Between these two functions there would be something like a layering, a sort of circular dependence of the soul upon the body and of the body upon

---

21. For any reasoning concerning the intelligible model, balance is of the essence.

> The accounts we give of things have the same character as the subjects they set forth. So accounts of what is stable and fixed and transparent to understanding are themselves stable and unshifting. We must do our very best to make these accounts as irrefutable and invincible as any account may be. (*Timaeus*, 29b; PCW, 1235)

22. One could thus ask oneself if the human does not thereby receive the power of realizing what the demiurge could only aim at, a perfect balance between the noesis and the noema, a pure objectivizing idealization of the model of the immortal gods. This is the theoretic invention of the concept—an indeed strategic invention, precisely as it has as its task not to satisfy the theoretic gaze through an act of contemplation, but to substitute a purely conceptual divine nourishment for the demiurge's potential failures. Its task will be supreme, since it will ultimately be a matter of conceptually maintaining the demiurge as a *survivor*.

the restitution of its soul. Each of its functions will constitute a particular type of assimilation and appropriation. The lactation of marrow, as we have seen, will provide the body of flesh with a force allowing it to struggle against, decompose, and incorporate the elements of the external world. The cogitation of the soul, for its part, will offer the demiurge the possibility of maintaining a resemblance between his representation of the world and the ideal model. But lactation inevitably becomes irregular, its flowing drop by drop becomes disturbed, contaminated with increasingly significant interstices. Cogitation for its part will not always be perfect; it will no longer be capable of spontaneously and systematically assimilating its contemplation with the object of its contemplation. The risk is thus extreme. For if the confusion of the soul and its object no longer occurs, if the soul no longer thinks of the gods *just as* the demiurge represents them, the demiurge will no longer be up to the task of keeping his promises toward the world; momentarily, he will no longer be the demiurge, his authority will be increasingly deposed, he will symbolically die, and the world in its totality will suffer an effective, indeed definitive death threat.

Before examining this nutritive dependency between the contemplation of the soul and the demiurge's mimetic promise, it behooves us to clarify that the soul will only absolutely cogitate, or rigorously objectify the ideality of the world, and thus develop as an authentic nourishment, through the disappropriating process of lactation. In order that the soul become contemplative, that is to say nutritive, it must not only free itself from the body but moreover—and especially so—free itself from it in a very specific way. When the soul thinks itself as the demiurge's representation, what exactly is it doing? What is it doing if not *reproducing* through thinking—or more precisely in the form of a thought— the demiurgic operation of the world recounted by the text of the *Timaeus*: not only the construction of the cosmic cycles, the revolution of the spheres and the proportional equation of the ideal numbers, but also the construction of the sublunary world by the lesser gods, the distribution of the animal species, the insertion of a body of flesh, and the unfolding of a process of death. In thinking the order of the cosmos in its totality between, on the one hand, the world represented by the demiurge and, on the other, the non-represented world, sacrificed and abandoned to the becoming of a slow but certain death, the soul will have to situate, define, and represent itself to itself as the *passage* from one world to another. It will have to reproduce this passage. It will thereby, through thinking, reconstitute the passage between, on the one hand, the process of death through spontaneous de-lactation, the internal deregulation of the irrigation of marrow, and, on the other, its own cogitation of the immortal gods. It will *itself become* the passage from one nourishment to another, between *milk-sperm* and the *ego cogito*. Furthermore, in taking it upon itself to become a nutritive link between two types of food, in giving itself the—specifically philosophical—means of becoming for its part the *concept* of this bond, the soul will constitute a *relation of representation*—which will define the essence and origin of every concept and objectivity—between the demiurge's noetic representation (the world as the starry heavens) and the purely phenomenal representation of the world (the irreducible becoming of time). And the universal order of the cosmos, its mimetic destiny, and the demiurge's promise would now, in some way, be in the cogito-nutritive hands of the human soul.

§3. With the sole goal of becoming the privileged food of the immortal gods, with the sole stake of maintaining the demiurge's representations in a *state* of representation, and thus consequently to guarantee a direct link between his representations and the immortal gods, the human soul will have to constitute itself in the shape of a gap between the two representations of the Universe. It will define *as a concept* both what separates phenomenal representation from noetic representation and what relates these representations to one another. As thinking milk-sperm, it can also define the specifically temporal irreducibility of the sensible world and the intelligible world—in other words, describe and conceptualize the limits of the demiurge's mimetic power—just as well as it can posit itself as the repetitive and reproductive substitute of these limits. The human soul, in fact, will have to suffer its limits and at the same time erase them. On the one hand, it will have the task of conceiving the demiurge's representation to the limits of his own power and mortality, of letting the demiurge know that his noetic representation rests upon an always already represented genetic order and therefore, as we have seen, that the cosmic time produced by his ideal aim will always already have taken place in the phenomenal time of this genesis, in the time of irreducible and disappropriating expenditure. In thinking of the immortal gods, in thinking of feeding them with its own concept, the soul will directly reflect upon the implicit risk of an illusion of the transcendental type: that the phenomenal representation reproduced by the demiurge must not relate to the *genesis* of the elements he represents—and therefore that the world as the starry heavens be nothing other than one of the demiurge's phantasms, the vain illusion of a dying god.

But, on the other hand, the human soul will make of this knowledge the erasure of every illusion—or, more precisely, the dissimulation of any risk of illusion. It will allow the demiurge to use this knowledge, to make use of it and thus to nourish himself from it precisely in order to guarantee the *mimetic link* between the representations. It will now become the (lacto-noetic) substitute of the demiurge's promises. It will take upon itself the demiurge's commitment, it will commit itself *in his place*, it will take the responsibility of the last of the guarantors in his place. So long as it can (objectively) *conceive* demiurgic representation in its own limits, between the two non-represented poles of its mimetic power, between the genetic temporality of phenomena serving as its ground and the omni-temporality of the immortal gods that serves as its model, the soul will guarantee the world that the demiurge is up to the task of keeping his promises, and thus *give reason* for [rendra raison à] the reason of the world; such is the cosmological origin of the λόγον διδόναι.

To take upon itself the responsibility of preserving the world in the place of the demiurge is both to ensure the proper functioning of the cycles of metempsychosis and put an end to the infernal continuity of their repetition. Once the human savagely gives itself to the desires of the flesh and the raptures of the soul, when it never or only very seldom thinks of the gods and the ideal numbers, all its thoughts will be mortal and nothing within it will subsist after the death of its body of flesh. The soul must now pay its debt; and thus begins the hierarchical cycle of metempsychosis, this dead time of the rebuilding and the choosing of a new body.[23] From the place of the man, the body will fall into the body of a woman, from the woman into that of a mammalian animal and so on to the slightest of the mollusks, the least philosophical animal on Earth. As Plato writes,

> if a man has seriously devoted himself to the love of learning and to true wisdom (τῷ δὲ περὶ φιλομαθίαν καὶ περὶ τὰς ἀληθεῖς φρονήσεις ἐσπουδακότι), if he has exercised these aspects of himself above all, then there is absolutely no way that his thoughts can fail to be immortal and divine (φρονεῖν μὲν ἀθάνατα καὶ θεῖα), should truth come within his grasp. And to the extent that a human nature can partake of immortality, he can in no way fail to achieve this: constantly caring for his divine part as he does (ἅτε δὲ ἀει θεραπεύοντα τὸ θεῖον). (90b-c; PCW, 1289)

Philomathy, philosophy, the love of truth and knowledge would thus represent the demiurge's last chances. Philosophy would thus not have as its sole concern and task the production of concepts and making of these nourishment *for the demiurge* (to think itself such as the demiurge represents it), but it will furthermore need, over and above everything, to assemble this nourishment as an object of worship, offered *on the part of and in the place of the demiurge* in memory of the immortal gods. For the human soul, to philosophize is to take upon itself the demiurge's responsibilities toward the world; it is to keep, in his place, the promise of never breaking the bonds of the world he mimetically organized. This involves a dual form of thinking. To philosophize would be both to *avoid the worst* and *play with the worst*. On the one hand, it is to prevent that the demiurge's representation be nothing other than a vain illusion, and thus spare the world the gradual dissolution of its constitution. But, on the other hand, to philosophize is to *posit the worst of all possibilities as possible*. Each time it thinks, each time it contemplates the gods represented by the demiurge,

---

23. On the process of metempsychosis, see *Republic*, X, 617e-621d; *Gorgias*, 524a-525c; and *Phaedo*, 113e-114b. Cf. V. Goldschmidt, *La religion de Platon* (Paris: Presses Universitaires de France, 1949), 75 et seq.; and Joubaud, *Le corps humain*, 262-79.

the soul can very well be mistaken and not conceive them as the demiurge represents them. The cogitative or cognitive error here would have immeasurable cosmological consequences: the risk that the worst comes, that the demiurge's authority be entirely withdrawn, that he be literally reduced to his own powerlessness and to the mimetic limits of his representation of the world, and thus that the account given by Timaeus be nothing other than a simple lie, and the rational order of the world, its λόγος, nothing other than a pure fable, a μῦθος. The world would live under the threat that the demiurge's noetic aim, clear and serene, become blurred, obscured, and finally increasingly confused with the phenomenal field of the linear becoming of the elements. The worst would thus have taken place. The worst of all possibilities would have taken place as world: and the demiurge will no longer be the demiurge, he would be symbolically dead, and the world in its totality would now be reduced to the fate of the body of flesh—a slow but effective death. And this is where the offering to the divine gains its whole meaning.

The body of the human (σῶμα), this body of flesh abandoned and sacrificed with the sole goal of saving the whole of the cosmos, would be the sign that the demiurge is himself, in his own way, a mortal and finite being. It would mean that the demiurge can lose his authority, his productive force (the proportional organization of the world), and his mimetic power (the representation of the world as the starry heavens). According to an orphic sense of death, particularly explicit in Plato's text, the body of flesh would be its *sign* (σῆμα), its *tomb* (θῆμα) and also its *salvation* (σωτηρία).[24] It would signify the demiurge's symbolic death;

---

24. On the σῶμα-σῆμα interplay and the orphic origin of the body conceived as a tomb for the human soul, see *Gorgias*, 493*a*, *Cratylus*, 400*c*, and *Phaedrus*, 250*c*. Cf. two articles by Pierre Courcelle: "Le corps-tombeau: Platon, *Gorgias*, 493 *a*, *Cratyle*, 400 *c*, *Phèdre*, 250 *c*," *Revue des Études Anciennes* 68, no. 1 (1966): 101–22; and "Tradition platonicienne et tradition chrétienne du corps-prison," *Revue des Études Latines* 43 (1965): 406–43. As Vernant writes, "the word *sōma*, translated by body, originally designates the whole of what within the body incarnates life and corporeal dynamics, it is reduced to a pure inert figure, an effigy, an object of spectacle and lamentation for others, before, burnt or buried, it disappears into the invisible." "La belle mort et le cadavre outragé," in *La mort, les morts dans les sociétés anciennes*, ed. Gherardo Gnoli and Jean-Pierre Vernant (Paris: Éditions de la maison des Sciences de l'homme, 1982), 65. See also, by the

it would pose itself as the sign-witness of its imminent, threatening death, be it indefinitely deferred, delayed, displaced by so many thoughts, knowledges, loves of truth, and philosophies. It would still be their tomb. The body of flesh would constitute the prolonged trace, the indelible mark where the imprint of the powerless and dying demiurge is inscribed. A commemorative body-stele[25] bearing the trace of the impossible, the demiurgic impossibility of perfectly assimilating the world to the ideal model of the gods. The body as a tomb, within a sanctuary-world (ἄγαλμα), will represent the site of this inscription and this terrifying moment of awaiting the concept, where the demiurge experiences the trial of the impossible and of his irremissible death—whence the idea of conceiving the world as the *tomb of the artisan god*. As long as the human will live, as long as its body will be fed drop by drop with the sacred sperm of lactation, the demiurge will die; he will be a dying being, he will himself now be, in the time of an infinite expenditure, he who dies in the movement of a decrepitude and dissolution without return.

---

same author, "Corps obscur, corps éclatant," in *Corps des dieux: Le temps de la réflexion*, ed. Charles Malamoud and Jean-Pierre Vernant (Paris: Gallimard, 1986), 22; and Joubaud, *Le corps humain*, 144–48.

25. As Vernant writes,

Its body now disappeared, vanished, what remains here below of the hero? Two things. First the *sema*, or *mnema*, the stele, the funerary memorial erected upon the tomb and that will remind the humans to come, in the following generations, of its name, its renown and exploits. As the *Iliad* puts it "still as stands [*menei empedon*] a grave monument which is set over the mounded tomb of a dead man or lady" (XVII, 434–35). Thus a permanent witness to a being that has, with its body, foundered into a definitive absence—and even, it seems to me, a bit more than a witness: once the stele, in the 6th century, comes to bear a figured representation of the fallen or that a funerary statue—a *Koûros*, a *Kórē*—will be erected upon the tomb, the *mnema* will be able to appear as a sort of corporeal substitute expressing in an immutable form the values of beauty and life that an individual will have incarnated the time of its brief existence. ("Corps obscur, corps éclatant," 34–35)

Cf. Homer, *The Iliad*, trans. Richmond Lattimore (Chicago: University of Chicago Press, 1951), 365–66. The relation between *mnēma* and the stele will also be found in the *Laws*, XIII, 958*d* (cf. Reverdin, *La religion de la cité platonicienne*, 116–24; Joly, *Le renversement platonicien*, 59–60; and Simondon, *La mémoire et l'oubli dans la pensée grecque*, 81–92).

The body of flesh can thus be defined as the demiurge's sacrifice. It will both represent the body abandoned *by* the demiurge and the immolated body *as* demiurge. It will constitute, on the one hand, the demiurge's salvation, the possibility of making a liberated soul the cognitive link between the two representations of the Universe, thus of maintaining a mimetic link between his representation of the world and the ideal model of the gods. And, on the other hand, it will determine the location of his own tomb, the inscription of an infinite awaiting, an awaiting that will nave nothing more to await other than the philosopher soul and, in its place, combine itself with the immortal gods. According to the *Phaedo*, to philosophize is to learn to die; it is to learn to await and, for the demiurge, to await the coming and the formation of the concept. In awaiting, in dying, indeed in agonizing drop by drop, it would be a matter offering the gods the substitute of something impossible, the iterably provisional and contingent replacing of this immortal form that the demiurge will have never been capable of adequately representing. Each time the human soul thinks of the immortal gods, it substitutes a body tomb offered in their memory for the demiurge's perfect representation. It will have done everything it could to keep their very memory in mind. It will have gone through all possibilities to safeguard in its memory, but also in their memory, and thus to never forget, that the demiurge's sacrifice is an abandoned body, delivered over to the infinitely reiterable duration of an awaiting.

Serge Margel is a researcher at the Fonds National de la Recherche Scientifique (National Fund for Scientific Research) and teaches at the University of Lausanne (Switzerland). For many years he has worked on the links among philosophy, literature, and religion in Western history. He has recently published *The Invention of the Body of Flesh: A Study in Religious Anthropology of Early Christianity; The Memory of the Present: Saint Augustine and the Temporal Economy of the Image;* and *The Autonomy of the Work of Art: Logic of Surfaces and the Avant-Gardes.*

Philippe Lynes is a Junior Research Fellow in the Institute of Advanced Studies at Durham University and has previously held the Fulbright Canada Visiting Research Chair in Environmental Humanities at the University of California, Irvine. He is the author of *Futures of Life Death on Earth: Derrida's General Ecology* and coeditor of *Eco-Deconstruction: Derrida and Environmental Philosophy.* Lynes has also translated Jacques Derrida's *Advances*, the original foreword to this book.